Shiva and the Primordial Tradition

The Linga of Gudimallam, second century C.E. *(Photograph copyright the French Institute of Pendicherry, used by permission.)*

Shiva and the Primordial Tradition

FROM THE TANTRAS TO THE SCIENCE OF DREAMS

Alain Daniélou
with Jean-Louis Gabin

Translated from the French by Kenneth F. Hurry

Inner Traditions
Rochester, Vermont

Inner Traditions
One Park Street
Rochester, Vermont 05767
www.InnerTraditions.com

Originally published in French under the title *Shivaïsme et Tradition primordiale* by Kailash Editions, Paris, Pondicherry

First U.S. edition published in 2007 by Inner Traditions

Library of Congress Cataloging-in-Publication Data

Daniélou, Alain.
[Shivaïsme et tradition primordiale. English]
Shiva and the primordial tradition : from the tantras to the science of dreams / Alain Daniélou with Jean-Louis Gabin ; translated from the French by Kenneth F. Hurry. — 1st U.S. ed.
p. cm.
Originally published: Paris : Kailash, © 2003.
Edited conference presentations and journal articles, 1938–1991.
Includes bibliographical references and index.
ISBN-13: 978-1-59477-141-5 (pbk.)
ISBN-10: 1-59477-141-3 (pbk.)
1. Saivism. 2. Hinduism—Rituals. I. Gabin, Jean-Louis. II. Title.
BL1280.522.D3613 2007
294.5'513—dc22

2006028258

Printed and bound in the United States

10 9 8 7 6 5 4 3

Text design and layout by Priscilla Baker
This book was typeset in Sabon, with Juliana and Avenir used as display typefaces

Note: Because classical Sanskrit diacritical marks were handled inconsistently in the original publication of essays included in this collection, the American editor has decided to dispense with them for all U.S. editions of this book. This decision in no way reflects upon Alain Daniélou's mastery of Sanskrit.

ईशा वास्यमिदꣳ सर्वं यत्किंच जगत्यां जगत ।
तेन त्यक्तेन भुञ्जीथा मा गृधः कस्य स्विद्धनम् ॥

ईशावास्योपनि॰

I—In a world where everything changes [where nothing is permanent] the divine is everywhere present [in flowers, birds, animals, in forests, in man].

II—Enjoy fully what the god concedes to you and never covet what belongs to others [neither their goods, nor their talent, nor their success].

Isha Upanishad, TRANSLATED BY ALAIN DANIÉLOU

Contents

An Introduction to Alain Daniélou and the Discovery of the Divine

Although on the one hand we may consider Alain Daniélou's discovery of India wholly fortuitous, on the other we may deem that he was particularly destined to do so, especially in view of what he tells us about his youth.

From an early age, Alain Daniélou was very unhappy in his Western Catholic circle. He launched into artistic activities, such as painting, singing, playing the piano, dancing, meanwhile showing deep contempt for "intellectuals" and detaching himself totally from Catholicism.

Throughout the twenties, Alain Daniélou certainly did not seem to be bothered about metaphysics, religion, mysticism, or philosophy. He sang and danced, taking rigorous and demanding dance classes at the Saulnier gymnasium in Montmartre along with the girls from the Moulin Rouge dance troupe. He gave recitals and lived a vie de bohème among an amusing artistic circle, with Henri Sauguet, Maurice Sachs (who had just left the seminary), and Max Jacob, for whom he had a great affection, while being totally disinterested in the poet's religious preoccupations.

At the same time, the family influences of his youth, particularly his mother's exacerbated Catholicism, were to have a decisive influence on the young rebel. Whereas his father had to be baptized so that he could get married, his mother, Madeleine Clamorgan, was very devoted to Pope Pius X. She fought firmly against the anticlerical government that had just outlawed religious congregations and set up first a substitute lay order called "Saint François Xavier," and then a school—"Sainte Marie"—where the values of Catholic ethics were very much to the fore.

Madeleine Clamorgan's brother was a canon, the curé of the church at Chaillot. Her eldest son Jean became a Jesuit and was made a cardinal by Paul VI, before becoming a member of the French Academy. Was the young Alain influenced by it all? He showed interest in some areas of mystery, although far from any official religion.

In the first chapter of his memoirs,[1] entitled "The Discovery of the Divine," he writes about a hiding place he created as a very young child in an abandoned nursery: "Here, alone, I could sense a mystery far greater than that of the ordinary human world." Yet again, reflecting on the priory of Resson, he wrote: "The old chapel held a strange fascination for me. I hated anyone else who came inside. I would stay there for hours on end, my mind completely blank. The red-shaded oil lamp threw dancing shadows on the wall. I was not afraid, though I felt an unknown presence beside me. I would perform all kinds of strange rites, which seemed guided by some mysterious force. I invented a complete ritual—was it really invented by me?—and as I lay flat on my stomach with my arms stretched out in the aisle, I would make a vow. I did not know what it was; when spirits exercise their will upon one's mind, they never express themselves through words. I vaguely sensed that I had been chosen for a special destiny and must pledge myself to it with no questions asked. That may have been my first real initiation. I was ten years old."[2]

His discovery of India was made accidentally during a memorable voyage crossing through it to reach Afghanistan, at the invitation of the crown prince, a friend of his youth, who was to become the king, Mohamed Zaher Shah. During this trip, he stayed for the first time at Shantiniketan, the school founded by the poet Rabindranath Tagore in Bengal. Daniélou, who remained very close to the poet up to the latter's death, was immediately fascinated by the world he discovered. His main interest continued to be the arts: dance and—above all—music. He became rapidly aware, however, that the circle around Tagore was already greatly Westernized. Little by little, he took an interest in the Hindu system, its philosophy and religion. Settling at Benares in 1938 was decisive from this point of view.

The declaration of war in 1939 trapped him in the ancient city of Benares. It was then that he decided to start studying under the pandits of orthodox Hindu society. He studied Hindi, Sanskrit, and music.

The influence of a great sannyasi, Swami Karpatri—who was extremely revered, especially at Benares, where his name appears in bold letters across the façade of a *math,* near the temple of Kedargath on the banks of the Ganges—was to be decisive. It was Karpatri who decided that Alain Daniélou should be initiated into Hinduism. The initiation took place a few years after his arrival in the holy city, during the course of a ceremony that was, as he mentions, "quite simple, like a baptism," without wishing to say much more. As part of the initiation he was given the name Shiva Sharan, meaning "the protégé of Shiva."

From this moment on, everything changed: Alain Daniélou, now Shiva Sharan, entered wholly into the traditional Hindu system, to the extent of judging any return to the Western world impossible. He discovered a religion totally opposed to the monotheistic religions he had come into contact with. He adopted all the Hindu rules. He rapidly became an ardent defender of this civilization and declared war on the later monotheistic religions, which he deemed to be pernicious and dangerous for the destiny of humankind. Their proselytizing, totalitarian, dogmatic character—unknown to Hinduism—appeared as a permanent source of conflicts, as recent history so clearly demonstrates.

Despite more than thirty years spent at his side, I always find it difficult to analyze his progress in the philosophic field (rather than use the word "spiritual," which he would not have liked). What is clear is that the more he learned from Karpatri, the more his conceptions of Hinduism evolved. Although he acted like a good Hindu, bathing each morning in the Ganges, and a brahman used to come each day to the palace where he was living to perform a ritual puja, Daniélou remained extremely modest and reserved about whatever concerned his own religious practices.

Alain Daniélou rejected Catholicism. His visits to Algeria and Muslim countries interested him on the musical plane, but never on a religious level, with the exception of an approach to Sufism during a visit to Iran and his contacts with René Guénon and Henri Corbin. His discovery of the Hindu world came upon him as an out-and-out revelation. This religion—as much a philosophy as a science—was in absolute harmony with his own vision of the divine.

Was his also an instinctive rejection of all kinds of prophets, spectacular rituals, masses, pilgrimages, and other gatherings of crowds under the pretext of religion? Did he not totally refuse to become a guide, a guru for confused Westerners in quest of oriental spirituality? Did he not consider the temple a place where qualified priests seek contact with mysterious powers and where the public has no function? Did he not accept the rites solely as a private relationship between himself and the gods, without witnesses?

The works he wrote, particularly his memoirs and the *Tales of the Ganges*,[3] denote a decisive orientation toward Shaivism—and doubtless toward Tantrism as well. Tantrism is, on principle, absolutely secret, so that we consequently know nothing. At the same time, Daniélou plunges with delight into every Shaivite text and many of his works allow us to discover concepts that differ widely from Vedism, the latter referring mainly to the four Vedas, about which he says very little.

Alain Daniélou sticks to presenting the theological and philosophical speculations of Shaivism, feeling that he has been designated for this purpose. He does not feel, however, authorized to teach secret practices, which Westerners lacking in spirituality would treat merely as exotic approaches. Shaivism is, at the same time, both the religion of the humble and of the most esoteric and secret currents of Hinduism. Daniélou was one of the first to present this religious thought, so little known in the West.

It surprises many, including many Indians, that his view in no way reflects the most visible currents of Hinduism, nor Western concepts of it, made on the basis of texts written—as a rule—in English. One example is that he gives little importance to the theory of reincarnation. He explains the meaning of rites involving animal—and even human—sacrifice, without pronouncing any moral judgment.

What is typical of Hinduism and evident from the view taken by Alain Daniélou is its tolerance, its total lack of dogma, and the possibility for each person to choose the way of life and religious practices best suited to one's own character. This is what Daniélou always did, making it impossible to classify or label him as belonging to any precise, definite current. A careful examination of his writings often shows apparent contradictions, which bothered him very little. Indeed, unlike most Hindus, he found theories about reincarnation just as questionable as those about paradise put forward by monotheists. He insisted on his decision to be cremated, which is by no means an absolute practice among the devotees of Shiva.

A realist, he considered that we are only the links in a chain, but that, if we do not take on this role, the chain will be broken, the line will be wiped out. He used to say, "We only continue in two ways: through our genetic code, meaning by procreation, and by transmitting knowledge, that heritage of learning that we can teach the generations that follow us." He also said, "We continue to exist only so long as someone continues to think of us."

One personal conviction remains and seems increasingly clear to me: Alain Daniélou, either as a natural gift or through contact with some extremely strong esoteric circle, had himself acquired powers—foreknowledge, the lightning glance, abilities that in some way made him a seer—but that, as a result of the orthodox education he had received, it was important for him never to show nor to use them except for wholly exceptional or serious reasons.

Did any other initiation take place, apart from the rite of his initiation into Shaivism? It is impossible to say. Some things are clear, however, such as his certainty of the extraordinary powers possessed by representatives of the esoteric currents he had met, which drew his admiration, as well as a distrust, or even fear, of the saddhus who so easily ensnare ignorant Westerners. He was also clearly opposed to the religions of the city: monotheistic religions, as also certain forms of Vaishnavism, which he found affected, sanctimonious, "plaster saint," just the opposite of hard, violent Shaivism, which is joyful and dissolute. The god Shiva, whom he identified with Dionysus in the ancient West, is a god of both life and death, the god of bacchanals and drunkenness, as well as of great austerities. Many of his books—such as *While the Gods Play: Shaiva Oracles and Predictions on the Cycles of History and the Destiny of Mankind* and *Shiva and Dionysus*—quote from ancient texts to explain the origins of this very ancient religion.

"Religions, taken as a whole, represent the most arbitrary and stupid speculations that man ever invented," Alain Daniélou told me, an argument he took up again during one of his interviews.

Whoever knows his work, much of which deals with religions and in whose titles the gods often appear, cannot but be astonished. Anyone who knew the man and his taste for paradox would recognize him immediately.

The first book that Alain Daniélou published, in 1936, was a collection of articles entitled *Le Tour du monde en 1936*.[4] From that time up to 1993, in addition to about twenty seminal works, Alain Daniélou wrote several hundred articles and papers for journals, encyclopedias, conferences, radio programs, and so on, some in French, others in English, Hindi, or Italian.

These texts deal with a very wide variety of subjects concerning India, such as its religion, society, language, yoga, and music. Some have never been published, and most are unobtainable. With his consent, and under his supervision, I began cataloguing these texts according to subject matter, whence the idea of publishing collections of these texts in book form.

Jean-Louis Gabin—who early on took an interest in this project and began working on it while Daniélou was still alive—has undertaken the task of writing the preface, as well as collecting and editing these various texts, which present a previously unpublished viewpoint of Alain Daniélou's work.

This volume particularly focuses on Alain Daniélou's writings about Shaivism, dealing with its primordial origins and its revival, its philosophy and practices, and its relationship to Tantrism, Buddhism, and Western philosophical explorations.

JEC

EDITOR'S PREFACE

The Ferryman's Task of Alain Daniélou

An essayist, musicologist, Sanskritist, and philosopher, Alain Daniélou was also professor of the Benares Hindu University from 1949 to 1953, honorary member of the Institut Français d'Indologie from 1943 on, Director of the Library of Manuscripts at Adyar in 1954, and member of the École Française d'Extrême-Orient from 1956 to 1960, before he became the director of the Institute of Comparative Musicology in Berlin and Venice up to 1977. In 1991, the Ambassador of India in Rome handed him an edict engraved on a copper plate making him the first Westerner to belong to the famous Sangeet Natak Academy. He passed away in 1994 covered with honors: the Légion d'honneur, Professor Emeritus of the City of Berlin, Commandeur des Arts et des Lettres (at the same time as Ravi Shankar, who dedicated to him the concert he gave on that occasion in Paris at the Théatre des Champs Élysées).

Daniélou has left behind him an exceptional work, translated and well-known in many countries, both in the field of comparative musicology and the safeguarding of "World Music" (the title of the collection of records he created for UNESCO), as well as in the field of Indian philosophy and culture. His bibliography includes books that have been classics for many years—such as his encyclopedic *Hindu Polytheism* (republished with the title *The Myths and Gods of India*); *Shiva and Dionysus; Virtue, Success, Pleasure, Liberation—The Four Aims of Life;* as well as *While the Gods Play*—works that have been translated, particularly in the United States, where they have been published by Inner Traditions or in the Bollingen series of Princeton University.[1]

If we add to these texts his scholarly translations in French from seminal Sanskrit and Tamil works, it is strange that his memory was not more honored by the academic world at the time of his death. In this regard, the *Encyclopaedia Universalis* was fully justified in concluding the long article devoted to him in 1995 with the words, "Bewildered by such a multi-faceted approach, university circles have mostly kept Alain Daniélou aloof."

What was Alain Daniélou's approach? It can be summed up in a sentence: For more than fifteen years, he practiced only Sanskrit and Hindi, immersing himself in the traditional society of India and its scholars, which gave him access to commentaries on texts transmitted orally, parallel to official Hinduism.

From this, it is easy to understand how far Daniélou was from ordinary university research patterns and, consequently, that what he can teach us is exceptional.

If Daniélou had access to texts and commentaries that are never—in traditional society—taught ex cathedra, and still less published, it is because he had no other goal than the research itself and was deemed trustworthy by those circles of traditional scholars and metaphysicians, who are similar to those who disappeared during the Middle Ages in the West and to those who may survive today in Sufi confraternities tolerated by Islam, which the history of mystic poetry tells us were often persecuted.

During his long stay in traditional India, which up to his last days he considered as his true homeland, Daniélou gradually acquired rules of life and ways of thinking that are very different from those of the society in which he was born at the beginning of the century. A rite of initiation marked the frontier, the second birth, of this Westerner who descended from one of the oldest families of Europe, related to

Shakespeare's "Dukes of Clamor." As he recounts with great humor in his memoirs, *The Way to the Labyrinth,* he was the son of a very Catholic mother, founder of a religious order, and an anticlerical father, several times a minister in the French Third Republic. His brother was a famous cardinal and he himself, to use his own expression, was "an apostate of some renown," who became assimilated into Hinduism, which does not proselytize and to which, in principle, one does not convert.

Such an adhesion to the object of research is almost unknown in the university approach, set on the "critical distance." His adherence can best be understood in the artistic domain, in considering Gauguin and his metaphysical Tahitian universe, which the colonization and the missions of his own time were busy destroying.

Daniélou's approach relates first and foremost to the traditional quest, which aims at identifying the seeker with the object of his search, or—if one prefers—of the initiate with knowledge. On several occasions in *The Way to the Labyrinth,* Daniélou writes that in India he sought nothing, neither career, honors, nor "powers." Just so, he sought nothing, except to understand a civilization thousands of years old, a traditional society similar to the most brilliant civilizations that are no more, which has remained intact, with its social structures, cults, metaphysical and philosophical systems, its arts, the fresh air of its diversity. As the Upanishads say—and this is something that he often quoted—"In all things, leveling means death."

Daniélou, who had practiced Western dance and singing at a professional level before arriving in India in the thirties, began by learning Indian music under a traditional master, with whom he communicated in Hindi. Since in traditional India—as in Pythagorean thought—music is considered the fundamental key to knowledge, Daniélou ended up meeting the scholars and wandering monks who always gather at Benares, the "heart of the Hindu world":

> After I had learned to speak and write Hindi fairly well, Vijayanand Tripathi, one of the great scholars of Benares, was kind enough to

> take interest in me and answer the numerous questions I had been asking myself. . . . Every evening, he taught from a raised platform in front of his house to a group of followers from many different castes assembled there. He had been the disciple of a famous Yogi and, besides classical philosophy, rituals, and interpretation of texts, he knew the most secret aspects of Tantric doctrines and Yoga practices. In his public lectures, he explained the episodes and the hidden meanings of the famous Ramayana in Hindi, written by the great poet Tulsi Das.
>
> It did not take me long to discover that this austere scholar had a completely open mind with whom one could discuss not only topics such as human sacrifices, omophagia, and erotic rites, but also the origins of language, cosmology, and Indian theories on the nature of the world, the atom, time, and space. . . .
>
> Little by little I entered into a mode of thinking so subtle, so complex, and so difficult that I sometimes felt myself reaching the limits of my mental faculties and capacity for understanding. I found myself immersed in a society whose conceptions of nature, of the divine, of morality, love, and wisdom were so radically different from those of the world where I was born that I had to make a clean sweep of everything I thought I knew. . . . This system of values could not have been more strange to me if I had been miraculously transported into Egypt during the reign of Ramses II.[2]

Literary people know well how difficult it has become to understand certain texts, such as Dante's *Divine Comedy,* or the *Roman de la Rose,* now that the traditional keys are lost, because esoteric knowledge was annihilated in the West in the fourteenth century, eradicated by an ecclesiastical institution crazed for temporal power—as Marguerite Yourcenar has so admirably shown in *L'Œuvre au noir*—an institution that did not, alas, restrict its inquisition to the frontiers of Europe.

That is why it is almost a miracle that a Westerner should have been able to renew this thread that was believed to have been completely lost. In this respect I wish to emphasize how decisive Alain Daniélou's loyalty has been in sharing with us the treasures he discovered. By this I mean that, on his return to the West, he never sought a musical career, for which his abilities made him well suited, any more than he wished to play at being a "guru" or "initiate," when it would have been quite easy for him to do so. Quite the opposite: He set himself the task of rehabilitating the traditional music of the whole world, not only of India, but of Morocco, Iran, and Africa, whose ancient traditions were threatened by ignorance—as always authoritarian and proselytizing—as well as by attempts to turn their music into folklore, or into study subjects, or to "modernize" it, as in the former USSR.

At this level, his success was outstanding. If Ravi Shankar or Ali Akbar Khan have been able to give their concerts in the same halls as Western classical musicians, if the art of traditional musicians and dancers has now been fully recognized for many years, without the slightest condescension, we owe it to Daniélou. As Ms. Noriko Aikawa, the chief of the Intangible Heritage Section at UNESCO, has clearly declared: "Today, 'music from far afield' has become a reference for many specialists and connoisseurs. These treasures have inspired many contemporary composers. We owe all this to Alain Daniélou. Today the existence all over the world, and especially in the Orient, of a music system which is as classical as that of Bach and Mozart, is universally acknowledged: we owe that fact too to Alain Daniélou's farsightedness and unstinting efforts."[3]

The results of Daniélou's approach concern not only musicology and Indian studies but also his literary creation: Two fictional works, *The Gods' Livestock* and *Tales of the Labyrinth,* provide us with a precise picture of the world of the wandering monks (saddhus) and the slightly less known world of the great traditional scholars of India. A quotation from his preface to *The Gods' Livestock* gives a glimpse of the universe behind his tales, in which, he warns us, all the characters are taken from life:

> The parallel world of saddhus, the wandering monks of India, is a world apart, and their function is to transmit, from age to age, the

> deepest forms of an immemorial wisdom, philosophy and traditional sciences. A major part of this knowledge is kept secret. The saddhus have, however, a duty to teach—wherever they happen to find themselves, even in the humblest of villages—the precepts necessary for the maintenance of religious and moral values. This is why Indian villagers have what seems to us a surprising level of culture as well as philosophical and theological preoccupations. . . . The world of the saddhus remains unchanged whatever be the transformations of the society around it. The saddhus are the representatives and wardens of the "eternal religion" *(Sanatana Dharma),* which is the primordial source of all religions. . . . The higher the rank of a saddhu in the monastic hierarchy, the more secret is his role and the more difficult it is to approach him. Perhaps at the summit of this hierarchy exists this mysterious and impersonal being sometimes called the *King of the World,* who can never be identified or located. Whenever the earth is afflicted by the folly of men, it is the duty of this Grand Master of the saddhus to instill in their minds the knowledge and ambitions through which they destroy themselves.[4]

Yet another—and no less direct—contribution of Daniélou's to the humanities is his elegant and accurate translation into French of several masterpieces of Sanskrit and Tamil literature, always carried out with the assistance of pandits: *Gitalamkara, l'ouvrage original de Bharata sur la musique,* the *Textes des Purana sur la théorie musicale,* published by the French Institute of Pondichéry, *Shiva Svarodaya,* the *Pièces de théâtre de Harsha, Shilappadikaram,* included in Gallimard's UNESCO collection, and *Manimekhalai,* published by New Directions in 1989.[5] To this significant list can be added the first unabridged and unadulterated translation of the *Kama Sutra* and its commentaries, carried out in the last four years of his life, for which—owing to the puritan heritage that the British left to modern India—he was unable to obtain the assistance of any pandit.

Throughout all of his work, Daniélou emphasizes the need to study the traditional Indian sciences, to translate them, and to ensure their preservation, starting with the ancient cosmological theories of Samkhya. He provides a considerable bibliography on these theories in his *While the Gods Play,* with the following presentation:

> We do not have the original texts of the ancient Samkhya, which was not in the Sanskrit language, but we are acquainted with its Dravidian terminology thanks, in particular, to the *Manimekhalai,* which is written in the Tamil language. . . . The teachings of Kapila, the dark-skinned sage who was the first to teach the Samkhya in the Aryan world, were collected by his spiritual heir, the magus Asuri. . . .
>
> Reconstituted and translated into Sanskrit at the time of the Shaivite revival, at the beginning of the Christian era, they were the cause of a prodigious renaissance that lasted until the Islamic invasions in the twelfth century. Only part of these texts has been published, and very few have been translated. Sumerian parallels have, moreover, confirmed their authenticity. The knowledge they reveal about the nature of the universe, the origin of matter and life, biology, astrophysics, the relations between thought and language, goes far beyond the most audacious concepts of modern science. . . .
>
> According to the concepts of the Samkhyas, the universe is made up of two fundamental elements, consciousness and energy. . . . Matter is merely organized energy. There is no material element that exists without being inhabited by consciousness. No element of consciousness exists without an energy-giving support.[6]

One of Daniélou's great merits is to have made these notions accessible to inquisitive minds, especially to Western scholars who are not satisfied by positivist postulates and do not know where to turn in order to find authentic traditional knowledge and science. In connection with this interest, it is highly significant, by way of example, that a mind like Hubert Reeves has given as an illustration to one of his most famous essays on astrophysics, *Patience dans l'azur,* the image of Nataraja (Shiva) dancing in his circle of flames.

Might it not be appropriate to make a careful and objective study of this notion of generalized interaction, at a time when genetic manipulation and alterations of the natural world, of which modern humanity deems it is both master and proprietor, have left the domain of theory and now invade the industrial market?

Greek cosmogony called our current era the Age of Iron, while Samkhya labels it the Kali Yuga, or "Dark Age." It appears that this era—in which totalitarian religions and military, economic, and bureaucratic dictatorships multiply and disseminate the means of destruction, poison soil, air, and water, and plant increasingly visible anguish in everyone's mind—is also to be the period in which access to knowledge is most direct and most rapid. In view of the libraries rising from the ground to reveal the forgotten civilizations of Sumer and Mohenjo Daro, perhaps the time has come to forget certain university prejudices, and publish and translate texts like those Daniélou has brought to the West's attention.[7]

This book offers the reader a glimpse into the vast world of Shiva and the primordial tradition, as seen through the eyes of one who not only studied it but himself became a part of that tradition. It brings together unpublished works, papers read at conferences, or articles published in journals by Alain Daniélou between 1938 and 1991.[8] In particular, the texts presented here focus on the prehistoric religious tradition of Shaivism, root source of both Samkhya as well as—with Jainism—modern Hinduism.

Many of the texts collected in this book deal with the various facets of the relationship of Shaivism with the Western world, an essential question, since the desire to restore such relations and the quest for primordial tradition was at the very center of the works of the medieval alchemists and those who initiated the Renaissance movement, such as Alberti and Pico della Mirandola.[9]

It may be useful to ponder why the quest for harmony, wisdom, and the transcendental unity of religions—which had animated enquiring minds in the medieval and renaissance periods—led, on the one hand, to a blind technological proliferation paired with the terrifying mutation of means of destruction and, on the other, to a standardized, anthropocentric humanism, which has already destroyed almost all traditional civilizations and now threatens the planet's very existence.

"In losing purity of heart, you lose science," wrote the alchemist Nicolas de Valois. It is this perversion of the search for knowledge—to which the semantic evolution of the terms "science" and "philosophy" bears witness—that holds the enigma of the violently profane character of the modern world, which does not appear to be a natural development from the ancient world, but rather a reaction to the traditional society whose degenerating social structures and religious dictatorships had straitjacketed thought.

Here it is important to point out—and the first text in the book affirms it—that "Shaivite philosophy knows no dogma. It does not separate theology and cosmology, science and religion. Their common aim is to seek to understand the nature of the world, and the role and destiny of living beings." Shaivism is consequently not a "religion" in the sense that we usually use this word; it only is so, literally, in its free and specific search for what binds human beings to the universe.

The structure through which Shaivism—whose very name was generally unknown to the French public before Daniélou's works were published—has been transmitted intact in India, with all its apparatus of seminal texts, preserved through long periods of apparent eclipse, is an initiatic institution: that of the sannyasis, wandering monks who are the repositories of amazing techniques of memorization and oral transmission, with whom Alain Daniélou was in contact for many long years.

Here, too, we must spell out our vocabulary. The sannyasis were—and still are—free men (and sometimes women) who have renounced earthly possessions and family life, though not necessarily sensual enjoyment, since, according to Tantrism, the "Indian cult of ecstasy," "the union of bodies in the act of love reflects the union of the cosmic principles and is perhaps our highest experience of bliss, of that limitless joy that is the nature of the divine."[10]

How can one not think of those wandering medieval alchemists, those "inhabitants of the universe," who abandoned their place in society to give themselves over to the mysterious "Art of Love"? Does not the symbolic conjunction of fire and water, as depicted in a Tantric Indian engraving kept in the library of the Sorbonne, represent the principal operation of the "Great Work"? Mircéa Eliade has already shown irrefutable convergences between tantric hatha yoga and alchemy, which both seek to deliver the mind through matter and matter through mind.[11] They both represent a search, a discipline aimed at transforming the mortal body into a "divine body," enlightenment through the discovery of correspondences between macrocosm and microcosm, the very vehicle of a research in which "beauty is the splendor of truth."[12]

At the same time, these studies are close to poetry, which is dealt with from various points of view in the texts that follow, such as "The Nature of Beauty According to the Samkhya," "Poetry and Metaphysics," "Music: The Language of the Gods." Shaivism's approach is diametrically opposite to the hatred of the flesh practiced by the religions of the Book, the murderous dichotomy of body and spirit, human and nature, which has tormented the whole history of the West in prisons and on pyres. This is here made very clear by essays such as: "The Symbolism of the Linga" and "Shaivism and Third Nature," which reestablish the metaphysical importance of what Judeo-Christian tradition has relentlessly inculpated and punished, and what a bourgeois society can only tolerate in the form of fourth-rate merchandise called: "pornography."

In the face of these trends we urgently need to hear the voice of Alain Daniélou reevoking the seers who tell us that: "In the microcosm, sex is the form in which the nature of the unformed is manifest;" and yet again, "because they evoke the primordial hermaphrodite, any sexually ambiguous being is of a sacred nature. . . . Every bisexual being can be considered as an emanation of the god's transcendent aspect."

The India we discover through Alain Daniélou is a country where stimulating contradictions coexist, considered as the very expression of the divine. Moralistic and puritanical Jainism prospers side by side with Dionysian Shaivism and its cults of trance and ecstasy. Vedism overlays

Shaivism and was influenced by it. Official religion allowed the parallel transmission of the occult to continue, and it is still the religion of the people and the earliest populations.

Buddhism disappeared from the soil of India as a result of philosophical contests. Nothing in the subcontinent's history remotely approaches the religious and ideological persecutions of Europe and America, or the racial and cultural genocides that are their contemporary equivalent. In these pages Alain Daniélou makes it clear that this particular fact is not the result of chance, but of absolutely scientific research and wisdom:

> Samkhya teaches that any method of investigation must first establish the limits beyond which its conclusions are no longer valid. . . . Samkhya has even been deemed atheistic, since it considers that the prime cause of the universe is non-spatial, and thus non-locatable, impersonal, and unknowable. Yet the representation of the energy principles . . . in the form of more or less anthropomorphic deities is part of a system used for teaching the masses and making accessible notions that are beyond their comprehension.

It remains for this presentation to indict most of the images and analyses of India circulating in the West as false. This subject, dealt with in all Alain Daniélou's works, is also tackled here: "Curiously, of India, the home of logic and the exact sciences, the modern West only retains abstruse speculations and irrational religiosity, neglecting a whole body of knowledge it would like to think of as being exclusive to itself."

The question of source material is essential. Alain Daniélou, who wrote and spoke Hindi and Sanskrit fluently, who had studied Tamil, was perhaps the only Westerner who was not only immersed in Indian civilization for more than twenty years but also was duly initiated and co-opted into the esoteric structures of traditional Shaivism. He was consequently a beneficiary of its prodigious oral transmission, certain texts of which he transcribed, which has inspired his whole work. Although some passages simply say in another way—which is also a way of making them clearer—what he has said in *The Myths and Gods of India* or *While the Gods Play,* other pages in this book are entirely new:

> Animals and plants are in some way the visible part of subtle beings, spirits, genies and gods, which govern and inhabit them. We can often make contact with the spirits through their vegetal or animal twin. This is why certain animals and trees are considered sacred. Through the respect and love we bear them, as well as their worship, we attract the benevolence of the subtle spirits, genies, and fairies that are their invisible twins, governing the aspects of the natural world.
>
> In this dualism of subtle spirits and animals, perception and knowledge functions are separated. In the human being, the divine game unites these two aspects; the human animal gradually develops an aptitude for knowledge, having in some way absorbed its subtle double, or guardian angel. This is why the human species bears a double heritage: its genetic, or physical heritage, which perceives external forms and delights in them, but is also part of the scenario; and its initiatic heritage of knowledge. . . .

To this he added the following note, specifically for publication with this book:

> The sacred is the telephone directory of the subtle worlds: The magic and the sacred are the two faces of the same communication theory. When we consider that the subtle beings are beneficent, we talk of the sacred, if they are evil or neutral, then we speak of magic.
>
> Nothing outside polytheism can properly be spoken of as "sacred." Sacred symbols, sacred rites, sacred places, sacred animals, sacred trees are inevitably linked to subtle presences referring to real and permanent entities that we sometimes disguise according to our mythological conceptions. Murugan, the infant god to whom children are dedicated, will become Krishna, or the child

Jesus; the sacred cave opening on to the entrails of the mountain goddess Parvati will become the place where goddesses appear, whether those of the Cretan labyrinth, of Præneste, or Lourdes.

Never has Alain Daniélou gone so far as he does in these pages in his revelations of such little known subjects as esoteric Shaivism, the personality of the great Shankara, Tantrism, the Third Nature, the Science of Dreams, or initiation.

JEAN-LOUIS GABIN

Shaivite Cosmology and Polytheism

Shaivite philosophy knows no dogma. It does not separate theology and cosmology, science and religion. Their common aim is to seek to understand the nature of the world, and the role and destiny of living beings. Seen from inside, the universe may be envisaged as a game, a fantasy born in the mind of a transcendent Being. But the Being that conceives the world is necessarily outside it: it is beyond the birth of space, time, and existence; it is unknowable, imperceptible, inactive, nonexistent; it is beyond number, neither one nor many. There is no way in which we can personify, imagine, or name this Being, except negatively.

This Being is that which has existed since before the creation of space, the receptacle that made it possible for the universe to be formed, followed by the explosion of energy that gave rise to matter, to atoms and suns, and to the measure of time.

MANIFESTATION

The first principle that appeared is space, called *akasha,* or ether, representing the development potential of the universe. Then appeared the plan, the system according to which the world develops. The laws of attraction and gravitation that led to the formation of atoms and galaxies must necessarily have preceded their formation, along with the principles of consciousness and perception. This set of laws, forming a preexisting image of the world, is called *Purusha,* the universal man.

Lastly, energy appeared, *Shakti:* the substance from which all the components of the universe are formed, whatever can be designated as "something" *(tattva)*. This mass of energy from which everything is fashioned is called *pradhana* (the base), or *Prakriti* (nature), but also *maya* (the power of illusion), since all the world's appearances are, in fact, merely more or less unstable combinations of tensions, or vibrations of energy. Matter is only apparent.

The Principle of Self

The first principle to come forth from Prakriti is the notion of individuality, of "self." Each atom, each cell, every living being, each solar system, takes shape around a sort of individual consciousness. A living being is merely a conglomerate of cells, each with its own individuality, its independent behavior, grouping together as a complex system around an "ego," something that says "I," which is, however, independent of its various component parts. It is the same for every atom, for every solar system, all of which are built around a consciousness of being, or individuality. A kind of consciousness is consequently present in each atom, in each planetary system. The sun has consciousness, just like every living being. This notion is critical, since the notion of a god, a divine personage, is a projection of the notion of individuality, of a being that says "I." Monotheism is merely the deification of the notion of individuality.

The Sixteen Tattvas

Then appeared the different components of which the universe is formed: the sixteen tattvas, that which can be defined as "something." They are the principles of what appear to us as the five states of matter *(tanmatra),* the five forms of perception to which they correspond, and the five related forms of action, to which is added the principle of thought.

The five states of matter first manifest as magnetic potential, then in turn in gaseous, igneous, liquid, and solid forms, while at the same time the five corresponding forms of perception appear. In the human being the five forms of perception are manifested in the five senses: hearing perceives vibration, touch corresponds to the gaseous state, sight is the fiery state and light, taste corresponds to the liquid state, and smell to the solid state. These forms of perception are connected to the states of matter: gaseous particles communicate by collision, by touch; the stars—which are fusion reactors—communicate with each other by means of light; liquefied elements mix or separate by taste, and so on.

Everywhere, in each atom, in each group of particles forming an entity, a "self"—the principle of thought—is present, together with consciousness, since Purusha, the plan, the universal intellect, pervades all aspects of Prakriti, or nature.

When we seek to understand the nature of the world, its origin, its raison d'être, following the stage we have now reached, we come across a more or less abstract aspect of what we term the divine. At the level of the principles of the five senses—the elements—we can envisage a god of the winds, Vayu, a god of fire, Agni, a god of the waters, Varuna, and we represent the earth that nourishes us as the Mother Goddess. The sun, the center of the world we live in, giver of light and life, is for us the very image of godhead. It is equally possible to envisage spirits that have no other substance than thought, like characters in a dream. We can conceive of gods that correspond to the powers of action, personifying strength, courage, justice, love, friendship, as well as destruction and death.

SUBSTANCE AND ARCHETYPE (PRAKRITI AND PURUSHA)

Underlying manifestation is the notion of Prakriti, the substance of the created world, considered as a female aspect, and the notion of the archetypal plan, which is Purusha, considered as a male principle. In Shaivism, this is the aspect represented by the phallus cult, the male principle from which comes forth the semen containing the genetic code, the plan of the living being, which manifests itself in the substance, in the egg contained in the female organ.

Here, however, our approach comes to a halt, because beyond the couple Purusha-Prakriti, or Shiva-Shakti, lies the barrier that separates the created from the noncreated, the nonexistent, nonbeing, the unknowable. We can only worship the world principle in its manifestation, its works. Whatever aspect of the world we envisage, we see in a veiled form an aspect of the divine plan. The divine work is, however, of an infinite variety. We can recognize the divine in whatever aspect of its work we choose as its image, in whatever we like most. Such an image may be a tree, an animal, a man, a woman, a bird, a stone, a symbol, or an idea. This is why the gods are without number.

All paths lead toward the Creator but never reach that Being. The strength of love, devotion, allows us to go a little farther each time, but our effort of concentration needs a support, and it is this support that becomes for us the image of the divine. We contemplate the face of the beloved knowing full well that that face is not the person we love. Similarly, the divine appears to us in multiple forms, in the guise of innumerable gods.

THE MONOTHEISTIC ERROR

Monotheism is therefore a metaphysical error, since the world principle, which is outside the world, is beyond number, impersonal, indescribable, and unknowable. Above all, monotheism is dangerous because of its consequences, since it is a projection of the human "self" into the divine sphere, replacing love and respect for the divine work as a whole with a fictitious character, a kind of heavenly king who governs human affairs, to whom the most absurd edicts are attributed. Intolerant, the so-called "only god" is, in fact, only the god of one tribe. Monotheistic religions have served as an excuse for persecutions, massacres, and genocides; they fight each other to impose the dominion of their heavenly tyrant on others.

In actual fact, monotheism is merely a political fiction. It does not exist on the religious level. We worship the Mother Goddess, the Earth Mother who appears in caverns. We worship different symbols, prophets, heroes, saints, and holy places. In our approach to the divine, it is not a matter of the image, the face that we give it. We can very well say, "It is in Jesus that I see God. For me, he represents that visible form in which I can best conceive the face of God." But when we say, "Baal is not god, let us destroy these idols," or else "Apollo is not god, God does not dwell in a sacred tree, the phallus is not the symbol of the Creator," we deny the presence of the divine in its manifested works. God is all. God is everywhere, or God is nothing.

We confuse what the Hindus call *ishta devata,* "the chosen god"—that aspect each of us chooses to worship as a representative of the divine—with the cosmogonic reality of the Universal Being. Our devotion toward our chosen god must not become a denial of other faces of the divine. We may well say, "For me, the woman I love is my chosen wife." But we cannot say to other men, "My wife is the only woman. You must make love with her." The error of monotheism lies in similar reasoning, opposing a chosen god to the thousand faces through which divine reality shines.

Who knows through what aspect of the world the experience of the divine will one day be manifest to us? For many, it is in the act of love that the lightning sensation of this reality suddenly appears. The union of bodies in the act of love, a reflection of the union of cosmic principles, is perhaps the highest, the most direct experience that we can have of beatitude, of the limitless joy that is the nature of the divine state.

The Shaivite Revival from the Third to the Tenth Centuries C.E.

Since prehistoric times, India has known two great religious traditions. The first, Shaivism, is a nature religion, which seeks to perceive the divine in its works and to become part of them. The second is Jainism, a humanistic religion, dealing essentially with ethical and social values. Aryan Vedism gradually incorporated the concepts of these two ancient traditions, at many contradictory levels, resulting in what is now known as Hinduism, whereas Shaivism and Jainism as such have continued down to our own times in parallel with Hinduized Vedism.

From Shaivism comes the cosmological research known as *Samkhya*, as well as Yoga, the study of the human being's latent powers. From Jainism comes the theory of karma and transmigration, which seeks to explain human inequalities as being due to moral lapses committed in previous lives, and justifies the social hierarchy on this basis. Buddhism and later Vaishnavism are adaptations of Jainism within the general framework of Hinduism. The Jain theory of transmigration has been used to justify contempt for the untouchables, making their past lapses responsible for their present condition. Buddhism carried this notion with it as far as Japan. Shaivism has never accepted the idea of the inequality of birth, even though it recognizes hierarchies at genetic, professional, and social levels.

In India, the period stretching from the third to the tenth century C.E.

was a period of crisis from the point of view of philosophic and religious thought. Buddhism had seriously shaken the foundations of Aryan Vedism, which had dominated India for centuries. Buddhism was, in its turn, contested not only by Vedism, but—more especially—by a return to the autochthonous religions. There was an extraordinary revival of a very ancient philosophic and religious heritage, coming from the prestigious pre-Aryan civilization, and in particular from Shaivism, from the cult of the goddess and the ecstatic and mystical rites of Tantrism.

During the course of history, the originally rather primitive religion of the Aryan nomads had assimilated many elements of the thought, rites, and cults of the great civilizations that had preceded it in India. However, it remained centered—at least nominally—on the texts derived from the Vedas. At the same time, these texts had gradually been reinterpreted and commented on according to the data of a much more developed philosophy, mythology, and cosmology.

The pre-Aryan civilization, which in proto-historical times had extended its influence as far as Western Europe, had not been annihilated by the invaders and had to a great extent continued to exist parallel to Vedism. The ancient concepts of Shaivism, Tantrism, Shaktism, and Yoga, together with the ancient Samkhya cosmology, lay beneath the surface and continued to reappear at every level and in every period. Owing to a historical aberration, there has been a tendency to present their reappearances as new developments, except when they have been envisaged solely in relation to Vedic civilization. Whether from the *Atharva Veda*, the *Upanishads*, or the traditional sciences, Brahmanism has constantly taken its inspiration from pre-Aryan culture, which little by little it assimilated.

The *Mahabharata* (XII, 349, 63, et seq.), referring to the leading religious and philosophical systems, mentions—on the same level—the Samkhya, the Yoga, the Pancharatra, the Veda, and the Pashupata, that is, Shaivism, Vaishnavism, and Vedism.

Throughout history, ancient Shaivism indeed remained as the religion of most of India's population, particularly in the south (which had preserved its original language), but also in the east, in Kalinga, Bengal, in central India, and in the Himalayan regions. Although the Aryans had installed missionary brahman families in these outlying provinces, they had never been really assimilated. They played a role of political as much as religious infiltration, rather like the role of European missionaries in the countries of Africa or Asia nowadays. Shaivite and Tantric rites, needing no brahmanic priesthood, continued alongside the Vedic rites, just as they still do today.

During the early centuries of our era, ancient Brahmanism—contested by Buddhism—lost its intransigence and adopted ideas of nonviolence, vegetarianism, and transmigration from Jain infiltration. Buddhism and Vedism both assimilated the practices of Yoga and Tantrism and adopted the Shaivite deities.

SCYTHIANS AND PARTHIANS

Between the first and third centuries C.E., the north of India experienced an extremely cosmopolitan period. Invaders from the north had established empires stretching from central Asia to the Punjab, Sindh, Gujerat, and as far as the Mahratta country and central India. The dynasties of the Pahlavas (who were Parthians) and the Shakas (who were Scythians) lasted until the end of the fourth century. The Yeh Chis, or Kushanas, who drove back the Parthians, came from central Asia, which always remained their true homeland. These newcomers did not belong to the ancient Aryan clans from which the brahmans claimed their descent. Since Vedism could thus offer them only a subaltern position, they were little inclined to accept it. They adopted either Buddhism or Shaivism and were sometimes even interested in Jainism.

Highly international, the Kushanas maintained cultural and trade relations with the Roman Empire, Persia, and China. Kanishka, the Kushan emperor who reigned from 120 to 162 C.E., officially adopted Buddhism, the propagation of which served as a pretext for his conquests, although his attitude toward other religions remained very liberal. Kanishka's coins show Greek, Zoroastrian, Mithraic, Buddhist, and even Shaivite deities (the last mentioned being mainly Shiva and Durga).

The Vedic deities had already been put aside. Kanishka's reign also saw—two centuries after the disappearance of the last Greek kingdom in Gandhara—the development of what is known as Greco-Buddhist art, but which is actually Indo-Scythian.

Kanishka undertook a reform of Buddhism to make it more eclectic and better suited to his political designs. He summoned a great council, during which the philosopher Ashvagosha, a Hindu converted to Buddhism, defined the canons of what is known as the Mahayana, or Great Vehicle. This work has a high philosophical content and is a kind of synthesis, integrating into Buddhism Shaivite and Tantric elements, as well as notions borrowed from the Greeks, Christians, Zoroastrians, and from the cults of central Asia. Having become the state religion, Buddhism set about absorbing—without too many upsets—the various religious tendencies of the empire.

This enterprise—which was highly effective from the point of view of India's cultural expansion in central Asia, Tibet, and the Far East—did not, however, succeed in India itself. The third century saw the birth, in southern, central, and northern India, of a revival of pre-Aryan culture, and of Shaivism in particular. This movement started in central India among a group of confederated tribes, whose chiefs were called the Barashivas. This was a reaction against foreign cults and modern religions like Buddhism but was also against Vedism. The movement was both religious and political, the revenge of a civilization oppressed for centuries by invaders who had long ridiculed it, at the same time borrowing the elements needed for their own development. The success of this revenge is a phenomenon that is almost unique in history. The Romans also took their inspiration from the thought and art of conquered Greece, but Greece itself never rose again.

The decadence of Vedism, followed by the discomfort of Buddhism, allowed the other non-Aryan sects to lift their heads and officially claim the position that had secretly always been theirs. Besides Shaivism, Jainism—that moralistic and atheistic religion representing an ancient autochthonous tradition—also regained a popularity that was previously challenged by Buddhism. Neither should we forget the influence that Jainism played in India and elsewhere. Jain missionaries had played an anything but negligible role in the development of Greek philosophy. The philosopher that Alexander wanted to take back with him from India, but who committed suicide shortly before the death of the conqueror, himself was a Jain. Buddhism had been a reform of Vedism mainly inspired by Jainism. In Hinduizing itself and integrating Tantric rites, Mahayana Buddhism lost its raison d'être in India, although puritanical Hinayana Buddhism offered an alternative to Jainism.

The new religion that arose, sometimes known as neo-Brahmanism or Hinduism, was not—like its predecessor—Vedism influenced by Shaivism but was henceforth Shaivism vaguely suggestive of Vedism, just as Mahayana Buddhism became Shaivism disguised as Buddhism. The texts and rites of Shaivism and Tantrism became the real basis of Hinduism.

Thus, after a long eclipse, ancient Shaivism—with its cosmology, Samkhya, its conception of the human being defined by Yoga, and its rites expounded in its sacred texts, the *Agamas* (traditions) and *Tantras* (rules)—once more took a dominant position, covered by vague references to the primacy of the Vedas. The term "Veda," however, was henceforth no longer understood as a "book constituting a revelation" (like the Bible and the Koran), but as meaning *dharma,* the universal law governing the world, whose various revelations are merely fragmentary insights owed to the intuition of inspired sages, the *rishis,* or seers.

The Vedic texts were no longer considered as revelation, but as a relative expression—among others—of the perpetual human search into the secrets of the natural world and the divine.

THE GUPTAS

In 319, a Jat, a Scythe from Rajputana, assassinated Sundara Varman, the last king of an obscure dynasty that had succeeded the Kushanas and reigned at Pataliputra—present day Patna—in the northeast of India. This Jat took power under the name of Chandragupta, founding a powerful dynasty that was to dominate northern India for three centuries.

This period, which was one of the most brilliant in Indian civilization, is sometimes called the "Golden Age of the Guptas." A period of peace and culture, it witnessed an astonishing artistic bloom, along with the production of many religious and philosophical texts that strove, with varying degrees of success, to renew the link with the most ancient traditions. This period is very much like what was later to be the Renaissance in Europe, as it was first conceived, the Renaissance of Prospero Colonna, Alberti, Pico della Mirandola, of the "Dream of Polyphilus."

Chandragupta's successor, Samudragupta, who reigned from 330 to 380, was a pious Hindu, who actively undertook to eliminate the foreign religions introduced by the Shakas and Kushanas. The ancient Shaivite culture, denigrated both by Aryan Brahmanism and by Buddhism, once more became predominant. Southern India, Bengal, and Kashmir, considered as the outer corridors of the sacred territory of India, had largely preserved the pre-Aryan cultural tradition that could now reaffirm itself. On the other side, the arrival of the Huns, who occupied the Punjab (toward 500), then the Turks, who closed the northern frontiers, isolated the Indian world almost entirely from its international contacts, particularly its close ties with central Asia and China. Only sea trade with Egypt, Persia, and Europe remained relatively active.

Chandragupta II, known as Vikramaditya, who succeeded Samudragupta, transferred his capital westward, to Ujjain. There, he gathered the greatest artists of his time, writers such as the celebrated poet Kalidasa, scholars like the astronomer Vaharamihira and the Buddhist philosopher Vasubandhu, and so on. Astronomy, medicine, and both sacred and secular architecture once more saw great developments.

TEXTS

This period saw the reappearance of a great number of non-Vedic texts, which had been secretly handed down through the centuries. Along with the sacred texts of Shaivism, the *Agamas,* and the *Tantras,* these texts also included Shaivism's historical books, the *Puranas,* whose roots—notwithstanding innumerable interpolations and recastings—go back to the dawn of prehistory. To these should be added the *Mahabharata,* that vast encyclopedia of knowledge. Some *Agamas* belong to different cults, which may or may not be connected to Shaivism. The *Mahabharata* commentary tells us that the *Agamas* are the sacred books of: the Sauras, the sun-worshippers; the Shaktas, who worship the goddesses; the Ganeshas, who practice the cult of spirits; and the Shaivas and Vaishnavas. The Vaishnavas consider the sacred texts of the Vaishnavite *Pancharatra* superior to the Vedas. These comprise some 100,000 verses, which have been adapted to conform in appearance with the Vedas.

Most of these texts are of extremely ancient origin. Echoes of them can be found in the *Atharva Veda,* in the *Upanishads,* the works of grammarians, and scientific treatises. How and in what languages they were handed down through the centuries is still a mystery. The Tamil versions of some texts are more ancient than the Sanskrit versions. Indeed, during the long period of Aryan domination, both texts and rites were handed down using the same method in use nowadays. Side by side with the bookish, exoteric tradition, kept alive by priests to ensure the continuation of the rites and teachings, the highest forms of knowledge are transmitted by the sannyasis, members of the monastic orders, whose initiation is essentially Shaivite and secret. They are outside the caste system and are hierarchically higher than the brahmans.

In such forms of teaching, the essentials of the doctrines are condensed into versified formulae, called *sutras* (threads), which can be memorized and handed down from master to disciple for generations, without leaving any visible trace. Such texts are even—sometimes—transmitted by persons who do not understand their meaning, merely acting as a kind of living book. At the time of the Shaivite revival, the heirs of this most ancient culture were obliged to produce their doctrines in book form in order to oppose those of Vedism and Buddhism. The *Agamas, Puranas,* and *Tantras* had to be transcribed in a form that was accessible to all. This is why many of these texts were drawn up in or translated into Sanskrit, which had become the universal cultural language. This at the same time discredited the Prakrit, the popular language utilized by the Buddhists.

It is impossible to understand Hinduism, or even the development of Vedism, without making any reference to that vast literature, which is—in actual fact—the basis of the philosophic conceptions, beliefs, and sciences of the Hindus. Often translated badly into Sanskrit at the time of the Shaivite revival, these texts have not received the attention they deserve. The fact that they have not survived in their original language or form has misled several modern researchers to believe that they were drawn up at the time of their new Sanskrit edition, whereas on the whole they obviously belong to remote antiquity.

By way of example, the fact that the name of Chandragupta had been added to the dynasties of the *Vayu Purana* led to the belief that this *Purana* as a whole had been written at that time. However, the *Puranas* are, by definition, historical texts, so it was quite normal to update them by presenting current events in the form of predictions. In fact, the astronomical references contained in the *Puranas* have made it possible to establish the extraordinary antiquity of some of the legendary accounts, taking into consideration that, at the spring equinox, the sun rose in the constellation of Orion in 4000 B.C.E., in the constellation of Taurus in 3000 B.C.E., and in the constellation of the Pleiades in the year 2000 before our era.[1]

THE DARSHANAS: PHILOSOPHICAL SYSTEMS

The philosophic concepts inherited from Shaivite tradition that were revived from the third to the tenth centuries were expounded principally in what traditional scholars know as the ancient Samkhya, the cosmological theory that studies the nature of the material and subtle world, seeking common principles behind the various aspects of existence, matter, life, thought, the archetypes of creation. To Samkhya, we must add Yoga, the study of the nature of the physical and spiritual human being, and Vyakarana, the study of language, instrument of knowledge and communication, whose limitations determine the possibilities of human understanding.

The theory of the six *darshanas,* or "points of view," on the basis of which any question can be approached, establishes a perfect balance between the different trends of philosophical, religious, and scientific thought:

> The Samkhya, or cosmology, studies the process by which the universe develops, according to archetypes of an essentially mathematical nature. The word *samkhya* means "measurable" or "numerable."
>
> Yoga deals with human nature and the relationships between the physical, sensorial, intellectual, and spiritual aspects of the human being.
>
> The Vaisheshika, or scientific method, studies the laws of the visible world.
>
> Nyaya, or logic, deals with methods of reasoning and the means of proof.
>
> The Purva Mimamsa studies rites and means of contact between the natural and supernatural worlds.
>
> The Uttara Mimamsa, or metaphysics, deals with the nature of the divine and human spiritual destiny.
>
> From the often-conflicting conclusions of their investigations, these approaches highlight the relative value of all knowledge and constitute a sure barrier against any kind of dogmatism.

Samkhya, Vaisheshika, and Nyaya, not being deistic, were taught side-by-side with Buddhist philosophy at the famous university of Nalanda. Toward the middle of the ninth century, Vachaspati Mishra published his great commentary on the darshanas, giving them the definitive form they have now. However, the Samkhya summarized by Vachaspati Mishra is merely one aspect of the ancient Samkhya. The main texts, such as the *Shashti Tantra,* are no longer accessible. The sole surviving texts are the *Samkhya Sutras* (attributed to the non-Aryan sage Kapila), the *Tattva Samasa,* and the *Samkhya Karika* by Ishvarakrishna (second century), this last work most probably being a summary used for teaching purposes. The initiatic and philosophic tradition handed down by the sannyasis, however, frequently refers to texts that have apparently been lost. It is difficult to know whether the original texts still exist outside oral tradition.

According to Samkhya theory, the universe developed from a nucleus, a genetic code whose characteristics are found in the structure of both atoms and solar systems, as well as in the principles of life, thought, perception, and communication. A sense of perception corresponds to each state of matter, and each has its own language, which enables us to conceive and convey an approximate expression of sensations and thought processes.

Thus, there is a language of smells (related to the solid element), a language of taste (related to the water element), a visual language of gesture (related to the fiery element), and a language of sound, articulated or musical (related to the spatial element or ether). The characteristics of these various languages are adapted to the multiple aspects of creation, to different life forms. The limitations of our perceptions determine our vision of the world. As with words, our sense organs are both obstacles and tools of knowledge.

The limits of language potentials form barriers to the development and transmission of knowledge. As certain modern linguists have remarked, one of the problems of contemporary science is to exceed the limitations posed by the concepts of Aryan languages. Sanskrit, however, has assimilated many notions that lie beyond the mental horizon set by Aryan languages, which explains why many Sanskrit words and concepts are so difficult to analyze and translate.

Samkhya teaches that any method of investigation must first establish the limits beyond which its conclusions are no longer valid. We find an echo of Samkhya conceptions at all stages of thought and philosophy in India, but as often as not, it is in scientific works that the cosmological theory is most clearly propounded.

The very ancient theory of language presented by Nandikeshvara in his *Kashika* and *Rudra Damaru Sutra Vivarana* explains language potentials and limitations as summarized in the hermetic formulas of the *Maheshvara Sutra.* This theory was to be developed in the fifth century by Bhartrihari in his *Vakya Padiya,* a work that has no equivalent in any other civilization, although the theory of the Creator-Word that derives from it is often mentioned, particularly in the Hellenistic and Christian world, but as a vague abstraction.

Applications of Samkhya concepts are found in rites, in sciences, in mythology, and in the systems of philosophy. However when such notions are isolated from the theory and its critical apparatus, which are only found in the commentaries connected with esoteric transmission, they sometimes give rise to aberrant interpretations and lucubration.

Samkhya has even been deemed atheistic, since it considers that the prime cause of the universe is nonspatial, and thus nonlocatable, impersonal, and unknowable. Yet the representation of the energy principles manifested in the different aspects of creation in the form of more or less anthropomorphic deities is part of a system used for teaching the masses and making accessible notions that are beyond their comprehension. Humans need gods, need an animistic concept that involves entities acting behind the subtle forces that rule the world. Thus, centrifugal force, the force of dispersion that gives birth to the universe, is symbolically represented by the god Shiva, the creator and destroyer principle. Centripetal force, bringing about concentration, coagulation, and the formation of material entities, is Vishnu, the protector principle. The resultant orbital force that presides over the formation of worlds, solar systems, and atoms is the god Brahma, the maker, or artisan. Similarly, deities also govern the states of matter: Agni, the god of fire, Vayu, god of the air and winds, Varuna, god of waters, without forgetting the earth goddess.

SHAIVISM AND VEDANTA IN SOUTH INDIA

The Barashivas and the Guptas opened the door to the Shaivite revival, particularly at a religious level. Later on, its great intellectual expansion was the result of the powerful Dravidian dynasties that took power in the south of India, where pre-Aryan culture had been maintained. The principal dynasties were the Pallavas of Kanchi, the Cholas of Tanjore, and the Rashtrakutas of Manyakheta. The Rashtrakuta empire, between 700 and 1000 C.E., stretched from the extreme south of the subcontinent to the Ganges valley in the north. It was in this period that the famous temples of Elephanta and Ellora were built.

Shankaracharya

At this period, we find many important men of letters coming from the south of India, who were of Dravidian language and training, but used Sanskrit as a means of expression. This was not without an impact on the development of philosophic thought, since the basic concepts expressed by the potential of the Dravidian languages are very different from those of the Aryan languages. The most important of these Dravidian scholars was—at the outset of the ninth century—Shankaracharya, the famous commentator of the *Brahma Sutras* and the *Upanishads,* founder of the exclusive nondualist school, the Kevaladvaita. After him came Bhaskara, the inventor of the theory of "separation in unity" *(bhedabheda),* which was later taken over by the Muslim Sufis. Next came Madhvan dualism, which is Vaishnavite, and absolute nondualism, the Shuddhadvaita of Vallabha. It was during the same period that Vachaspati Mishra's commentary on the *Yoga Sutras* by Patanjali appeared.

At a philosophical level, Shankaracharya can be considered as the person who definitively annexed Vedism to Shaivism, utilizing a subtle and often perverse dialectic, as well as terminological artifices to carry the notions of one system into the other.

Born in Kerala, in southern India, Shankaracharya was initiated as a sannyasi when he was very young, without having first passed through the obligatory stage of marriage. A man of any caste can become a sannyasi. He then changes his name and his origins must be kept secret. It was later claimed that Shankara was the posthumous son of a brahman, and had been raised by his widow. He was the disciple of a certain Govinda, himself the disciple of Gaudapada who, in the seventh century, had commented on the *Samkhya Karika* and had also written a commentary on the *Mandukya Upanishad.*

In his masterly commentaries on the *Brahma Sutras,* on some of the *Upanishads*, and on the *Bhagavad Gita*, Shankara strove to provide a synthesis of the ideas of the Shaivite Samkhya, Jainism, Buddhism, and elements from the various Darshanas. That hard and systematic brain whose mother tongue was Dravidian developed an extremely logical philosophical doctrine in an irreproachable, scholarly Sanskrit. Under the name of Vedanta, this doctrine was to pass for a synthesis of Hinduism, whereas the very principle of the Darshanas was to seek different approaches and combat any kind of simplification or synthesis.

The ancient Samkhya—which, as we have seen, is a prudent search for a certain number of fundamental realities known as tattvas, or "basic elements"—is much less dogmatic than the Vedanta—which, in seeking to synthesize, destroyed a complex system of investigations into the nature of the world and the divine that had made it possible to coordinate scientific research and metaphysical speculation without confusing them.

Indeed, Shankara is one of the first inventors of what in modern terms is known as an ideology, that is, a logical system with scientific claims, developed using skillful dialectic, but with assumptions that do not necessarily correspond to reality, inevitably leading to unhappy experiences. Not without reason, Madhva defined Shankara as "a deceitful demon who has falsified the teachings of the *Brahma Sutras* to lead souls astray." Shankara's work, however, remains important for his skillful demoralization of the religious hegemonies set up by Vedism and Buddhism. Thus we might speculate on the deeper motives of this great philosopher.

The Evolution of Vedanta

Starting from the seventh century, there was a revival in the activities of the ancient churches of Kerala, a region that also contained a Jewish community who, deported by the Phoenicians, had settled there beginning in 555 B.C.E. Born in Kerala, Shankara could not have been ignorant of the existence of these Jewish and Christian communities. At the same time, the widening influence of Islam was giving rise to serious intellectual and religious problems. The Arabs had occupied Kabul in 650, and the Sindh a little later on. The conception of monotheism, along with its aggressiveness and the audacity with which such a simplistic doctrine could be presented as progress, impressed the philosophers, who sought to adapt it, interpret it, and incorporate it. It was a phenomenon like Marxism, which clandestinely penetrated all religious thought, no one daring to point out the countertruths and the unrealistic nature of its assumptions.

The prestige of the metaphysical absurdity that monotheism represented for traditional doctrine was to affect philosophic thought in India down to our own times. The Western world was hardly interested in anything but philosophies infected by this germ. In vain, the *Tantras* continued to proclaim "*ekashabdatmika maya:* the number 'one' is the soul of error." For the Samkhya, the number "one" is collective, referring to a group or fragment, and does not exist as an absolute, since nothing exists except in relation to something else.

The wise and prudent cosmology of the Samkhya—which, starting from the sentiment of the omnipresence of the supernatural derived from animistic concepts, goes back through the subtle energies, personalized by the major Shaivite, Vedic, and Buddhist gods, to arrive at a nonspatial, impersonal, and unknowable prime cause—found itself faced with the simplistic theory of a personal artisan-god who made the world, governs it arbitrarily, and dictates rules of conduct directly to humanity.

The most primary ideas are the ones that most easily disarm philosophers. They search for ambiguous explanations to tackle them and incorporate them in one way or another in traditional philosophy. The problems raised in India by confrontation with Islamic and Christian monotheism certainly played a role in the importance given to nondualist or more-or-less monist speculations.

Identifying Atman with Brahman, that is, identifying the center of the human being with the prime, nonmanifested cause of the universe, beyond space and time, does in fact imply a personification, a spatial localization of Brahman, and justifies the eventual divinization of incarnations. Identifying the soul, conceived as the center of the living being, with a nonmanifested Absolute is, however, a contradiction of terms. Brahman, envisaged by the Samkhya as the prime cause, neutral, impersonal, and unknowable, in actual fact becomes, without it being admitted, an only god, easily personified, close to the Christian and Muslim concept.

Under the name of Vedanta, the Uttara Mimamsa, thus tastefully brought up to date, was to become of great importance, almost leading to the elimination of the other Darshanas. Having lost its own critical apparatus, the Vedanta was to become purely speculative. Its apparent rationalism would attract thinkers in the Christian and Islamic world, with the result that it obtained a sort of exclusivity as representing philosophic thought in India.

Curiously enough, of India—the home of logic and the exact sciences—the modern West was to retain particularly its abstruse speculations and irrational religiosity, thus neglecting a whole body of scientific and philosophic knowledge, which they preferred to attribute to themselves.

In our own time, in India as in the West, the emphasis laid on the Westernized Vedanta to the detriment of much more concrete forms of thought makes the modern approach incomprehensible to traditional Hindu scholars, used to the rigorous disciplines of the Darshanas and to the scientific and cosmological concepts of the Vaisheshika and Samkhya. I had the chance to ascertain this fact when, as advisor to the traditionalist Hindu party,* I was often questioned about the importance that Westerners attributed to the philosophy of Aurobindo and to the theories of Gandhi, which to them seemed unbelievably elementary and puerile.

Anchored to its notion of progress, the modern world tries to see as a new development what is often merely a distortion or decadence of thought, or merely a reference to an unexplained system. The lucubration and disputes between monism, nondualism, qualified nondualism, dualism, and so on are the result of the problems raised by Christian and Islamic monotheism, which Hindu philosophy had to tackle.

Westernized Vedanta has become the basis of that syncretism sought by modern thinkers, like Ramakrishna, Aurobindo, and Gandhi. In actual fact, it represents the elimination of the scientific and logical

---

*The Ram Rajya Parishad founded by Swami Karpatri in 1948.

spirit of the Samkhya that, corrected by the other Darshanas, accepts any hypothesis as necessarily relative, and finds in the very contradiction of the conclusions a critical method that avoids any commitment to blind belief, arising out of illusory simplification.

THE REVIVAL'S IMPACT ON THE WEST AND FAR EAST

From the point of view of philosophical and religious thought, the arts and sciences, from the third to the twelfth centuries, India was the unrivalled center of civilization and humanism. It could not have failed to have an impact on other world cultures. Probably Indian architects, driven from present-day Afghanistan by the Islamic invasions, took part in the rise of the West's cathedrals, just as they did in the building of Islamic monuments. We shall never fully understand the Middle Ages in the West if we do not take into account the influence—despite the distance and obstacles—that Indian culture, then at its height, must have exercised over medieval Europe.

The intellectual effervescence that made India the center of religious and philosophic thought between the third and tenth centuries only concerned the rather limited world of scholars. It involved discussions of ideas, philosophical jousts in a refined society, rather than profound religious movements. Somewhat like in the Greece of the classical period, a number of schools developed and fought each other. Some have left little trace.

Modern Orientalists have shown little interest in the scientific aspects of the knowledge of those periods, even though atomic theory, the theory of the relativity of space and time, mathematical theories, astronomical and geographic attainments, the theory of gravity, were all much in advance of anything the Western world could then offer.

For example, in the middle of the fifth century, the astronomer and geographer Aryabhata gives us a description of the terrestrial world, including the vast Antarctic continent (whose inhabitants' heads are upside-down as compared to those of the North Pole, but they are unaware of the fact), indicating the precise time difference between New

Guinea, Ceylon, and a city on the American continent, apparently in Guatemala or Mexico, called Siddhapura, the City of the Perfect.

Cultural exchanges between India and the Chinese world have always been very important but are little known, since they were at the level of the Samkhya, the sciences and Tantrism, never at the level of Vedism. From an Indian point of view, such exchanges are mentioned starting from a very ancient period, especially as concerns magical and Tantric rites. Often, the *Tantras* recommend using the "Chinese rite" or *chinachara* for certain practices. We know little of the influence of Jainism in China, although it is highly probable. Mahayana Buddhism added a new dimension to these exchanges. The first Buddhist missionaries reached China in 160 C.E. Tibet adopted Mahayana Buddhism. Henceforth, Buddhist missionaries ensured constant contacts between the civilizations of India and China. Chinese travelers visited India at various times. Fa Hsien stayed at the court of Vikramaditya Gupta from 399 to 414, where he probably met the poet Kalidasa. Hiuen Tsang stayed at the court of Harsha from 629 to 645 and has left an important account of his journey.

During the Shaivite revival, the Samkhya once more attracted the attention of Chinese thinkers. Gaudapada's commentary on the *Samkhya Karika* by Ishvarakrishna was translated into Chinese in the sixth century. Texts on the atomic theory of the Vaisheshika were translated in 648, as were Kanada's *Sutras*.

THE RELIGIOUS REALITY

Apart from the philosophers' speculations, which only concerned a small group of intellectuals, what was the actual religion in India during this time? There was an amazing mosaic of rites and beliefs, whose unity lay in diversity. India was, and still is, a tolerant country. Neither the political imposition of Buddhism nor the missionary fanaticism of Muslims, Christians, and—later on—Marxists were able to seriously undermine this diversity.

The tribes remained animist, propitiating the spirits, the *bhutas*, which animate the natural world, living in trees and peopling ponds and rivers. The language of these tribes, continuing down to our own times in the Munda dialects, is a survival of the most ancient layer of prehistoric civilization on the Indian subcontinent, related to the Australians and the Pygmies in Africa.

Besides the tribes, as a whole, the people of Dravidian or Aryanized languages remained Shaivite and practiced Tantric and magical rites and sacrifices. Yoga remained the method of development and progress of the human being. The cosmology of the Samkhya was the basis of scientific and philosophic concepts.

Buddhism, gradually assimilated by Shaivism, was eliminated little by little, except in Ceylon and Nepal. Vedism, respected but profoundly transformed, continued as the basis of the official rites handed down by the brahmans, but its gods no longer had any place in popular religion. The cult of deified pre-Aryan heroes, mainly Krishna and Rama—declared to be incarnations of Vishnu—replaced the ancient gods worshipped by the people.

Only Jainism, that other great pre-Aryan religion, maintained its integrity, its basic atheism, its theories of nonviolence and reincarnation, its vegetarianism, and strict moralism.

The Sects

Starting from the fourth century, a great number of Shaivite, Vaishnavite, animist, or atheist sects reappeared in the light of day, having been freed from ostracism and the clandestine existence to which they had been relegated by the Vedic, then Buddhist, state religions. Each had its own sacred books, its *Agamas,* presenting a body of religious and philosophical concepts of astonishing richness and variety. Some of these sects have survived, while others have now disappeared. The same is true of their books, destroyed or eaten by bookworms in little-known and badly-kept libraries for over a thousand years, ever since the Muslim and later European invasions struck a serious blow at the cultural organization and freedom of thought of the Hindu world. Essential principles are, however, preserved by oral tradition.

Among the most important sects active between the second and tenth centuries, we should mention the Sauras, the sun-worshippers, who deemed that the earth and other planets come from that star and that there is nothing on the terrestrial world that does not exist in the sun. The sun is thus the principle, the origin of matter, as well as of life, thought, and consciousness. The solar system is a living, thinking, conscious cell.

The Saumias, on the other hand, worshipped *soma,* the sacred liquor of the Vedas. The moon is a cup of soma, which nourishes the gods. Soma, the essence of life and elixir of immortality, is also represented by human seed, the source of life.

The Ganapatyas worship the *ganas,* the boisterous and delinquent juvenile spirits who are Shiva's companions, as well as Ganapati, the elephant-headed god who is their chief. Nothing must be attempted without ensuring the benevolence of the ganas. This is why, down to our own times, Ganapati's image is placed above the house door.

The Pashupatas form one of the major Shaivite sects. Their doctrine is known as Shaiva Siddhanta and is attributed to Lakulisha, who is deemed to be an incarnation of Shiva-Pashupati, the lord of the animals. The word *pashu,* animal, also includes the human animal. This doctrine envisages three principles: *pati,* the master, pashu, the herd, and *pasha,* the snare, that is, the bond of natural forces and laws by which the master keeps the herd in his power. This sect practices violent rituals, sacrifices mixed with screams, laughter, and dances, that are very close to the Dionysian rites.

By contrast, within the Vira Shaiva sect there developed a kind of abstract and moralistic vegetarian Shaivism, influenced by Jainism. It has many followers in southern India. We should also mention the important revival of the cult of Skanda, Shiva's son, identified with Murugan, the young prehistoric god of the Dravidians, whose legends are identical to those of Cretan Dionysus.

The prehistoric cult of the goddesses also reappeared forcefully and is still the popular religion of Bengal today. The ancient cult of the *nagas* (snakes)—who are considered to be the race that preceded humankind and now live in a subterranean world—must also have played a very important role if we go by the number of naga images in temples of the Gupta period and even later on, in what is called the medieval period.

At the same time, materialistic and atheistic movements reappeared, such as the Nastikas (without god) and the Lokayatas (materialists), one of whose champions was the famous Charvaka, who considered thought to be a fermentation of matter, and denied the existence of the supernatural and the survival of the soul.

At the same time, toward the fifth century, western India, though still under Scythian dominion, saw the renaissance of a form of Vedism that was very strict at a social level—particularly as far as the castes were concerned—while quite liberal on the religious level. This revival, together with the rise of Shaivism, ultimately led to the final defeat of Buddhism in India. Indeed, assimilated Scythes, such as the Rajputs and the Mahrattas, have always felt close to the original Aryans. They have played a major role in reasserting Vedism down to our own times, although the authenticity of their Aryanism has been—and still is—contested by the other brahman dynasties. This is one of the arguments that have recently been used to criticize, from the Hindu point of view, the *Arctic Home of the Vedas,* the great work by Tilak, who was a Mahratta.

Bhakti

One important development was that of the devotional and ecstatic cults with regard to what is known as *bhakti.* The Bhagavatas or Pancharatras (devotees and scriptures dedicated to Vishnu) worshipped the pre-Aryan heroes and in particular Rama and Krishna, considered thenceforth as incarnations of Vishnu. Vishnu is the male equivalent of the principle that the Shaivites call Shakti, the goddess. There is thus an affinity between Shaktas and Bhagavatas. From this tradition comes the notion of bhakti, devotion, total surrender of the self, considered as the most effective means of approaching the divine.

The fundamentally anti-intellectual cult of Bhakti spread rapidly during the Muslim period, giving rise to the flowering of devotional poetry, both in Sanskrit and in the popular languages. The Alvars, the Vaishnavite saints of the south, had already produced a vast mystical literature in Tamil, which came to exercise a great influence on Indochina and Indonesia. At the same time, the Nayannars, other Tamil saints who were Shaivite, transposed this mystical tradition into Shaivite terms. Their songs were spread by wandering devotees. In the north, Chaitanya, Kabir, Mirabai, Surdas, and others are famous examples. Those orange-robed scatterbrains now rampant on the streets of New York, Paris, and Berlin belong to this tradition.

Bhakti, that sentimental religious feeling toward an ill-defined and humanized deity, ignored all metaphysical problems and made great strides in the periods of disarray that followed the Islamic invasion. It has evident equivalents in the Christian world. Parallel to a simplified Vedanta, Bhakti, Krishnaism, and fanatical deistic sects developed, which have purveyed a strangely distorted image of Hindu philosophy and religious and metaphysical thought.

At a devotional level, Shia Islam and Hindu Bhakti are akin in confusing the neutral, abstract creator principle with a personal god. Close relations were established between Indian and Persian mystics. The doctrine of "separation in unity" *(bhedabheda vada),* defined by Bhaskara in the eighth century, was taken up by the Muslim Sufis. The ecstatic practices of both Bhaktas and Sufis are identical, just like the mystic exaltation of the *qataris,* the wandering Muslim poets, and the Hindu *kajari* singers. These pious nomadic musicians still today sing both qatari and kajari poems, particularly those of Kabir.

CONCLUSION

It was this highly diversified world, with total freedom of thought and belief, that saw the development—from the third to tenth centuries C.E.—of one of the most astonishing periods of art, philosophy, and religious life in India, one of the most remarkable moments in the history of humankind, up to the day when the Muslim hordes destroyed its temples and broke its growth. It took a whole series of Islamic invasions, with the ferocious destruction that accompanied them, to paralyze a civilization that was the most developed in the world for its thought, science, and arts, and amazed both Western and Chinese visitors at that time.

The methods that allowed Hinduism to survive the worst vicissitudes continued to be effective, despite Western, Islamic, Christian, and Marxist intrusions. As it is now lived, at the level of beliefs and rites as well as philosophical concepts, Hinduism has not changed since it came into being at the time of the great Shaivite revival in the Golden Age of the Guptas. Traditional society prudently remains, however, on its guard, and for foreigners and Westernized Indians, access to true Hinduism remains very difficult.

At a time when the scientific and metaphysical thought of the West is drawing remarkably close to the concepts of Samkhya, as in the case of the so-called Gnostics of Princeton, and when the very notion of polytheism has ceased to be taboo, the attraction found by many young people for Bhakti and mystic wandering is perhaps a prelude to a return to a conception of human and divine, of love and what is sacred, that is close to those Shaivite concepts whose rediscovery gave birth to the prodigious flowering of culture, art, and thought that characterized Indian civilization from the third to the tenth centuries of our era.

The Symbolism of the Linga

The symbol of Shiva, the Creator of the world, the image worshipped in his temples, is the erect phallus, the *linga*. It is gripped in the female organ, the *yoni,* but does not penetrate it. It rises victoriously out of it, like the column of fire that rises from the earth's entrails, known as the Linga of Light. The *Shiva Purana* tells us that "The word *linga* means sign; the distinctive sign through which the nature of something can be recognized is called linga."[1] It also states that "The god Shiva himself is in reality without any sign (without any sexual organ), without color, without taste, without smell, beyond the reach of words or touch. He is without qualities, immutable, immobile."[2]

The *Linga Purana* adds: "In the abstract, in which there is no distinguishing sign, appears a sign that is the universe. This sign can be mentioned, touched, breathed, seen, tasted. It is the origin of gross and subtle elements."[3]

The godhead can only be perceived through its creation, which is its sign, its linga. Its image is omnipresent in its work. In the microcosm, meaning the human being, the sexual organ, the source of life, is the form in which the nature of the abstract is manifest. However, the *Shiva Purana* says that "it is not the phallus itself that is worshipped, but he of whom the phallus is the sign, the Progenitor, the Cosmic Being. The phallus is the emblem, the sign of the person of Shiva, of whom it is the image."[4]

This is elucidated by Swami Karpatri in his *Lingopasana Rahasya:* "The symbol of the Cosmic Man, Purusha, the plan of the universe, present in all things, is the male emblem, the linga. The symbol of Energy, which is the substance of the world, the generative force of all that exists, is the female organ, the yoni."[5]

"The center of pleasure is located in the sensual organ *(upastha),* in the phallus and the yoni, whose union is the essence of all enjoyment. All love, all sensuality, all desire, is a search for enjoyment. The godhead is an object of love only because he represents undiluted sensual enjoyment. All enjoyment, all pleasure, is an experience of the divine. The whole universe gushes forth from the enjoyment."[6]

THE LINGA OF LIGHT

The principle called Shiva can be represented as the axis of world manifestation, which develops starting from the limit point, the *bindu,* the point from which the universe arises. This world axis is represented as a pillar of light crossing the universe from top to bottom.

In Yoga, the "subtle center located at the base of the spine is a triangle of desire, knowledge, and action forming the yoni, in the center of which rises the linga born-of-itself, shining like a thousand suns."[7]

The principle called Shiva represents all the procreative power of the universe. According to the *Shvetashvatara Upanishad,* "It is he alone who penetrates all matrices." Swami Karpatri elaborates:

> The universe is the outcome of the relation of a linga and a yoni, of a form and a substance. Everything consequently bears the signature of the linga and the yoni. It is the deity who, in the form of the individual phallus, penetrates each matrix and procreates all living beings.[8]
>
> In the sun, we worship the dispenser of light, the sum of all eyes. Similarly, in the phallus, we worship Shiva, present in all procreative power. It is not any particular eye that we worship and of which we make images, but the sun, the total eye that gives us sight, the source of visibility. Similarly, it is the entire Shiva that is worshipped, of which images are made.[9]

And, according to the *Skanda Purana,* "Space is the linga, the earth is his altar. In him reside all the gods. He is the sign, because everything dissolves in him."[10]

SEED: *BIJA*

Sperm is the seed *(bija)* of life. It is the best of oblations, the purest form of sacrificial elixir *(soma)*. All beings are born from the offering of sperm thrown into the fire of desire. Agni, the lord of fire, is portrayed drinking the sperm that shoots from Shiva's phallus. The moon is the cup of soma, of sperm, that Shiva wears on his forehead.

Sperm is called bija (seed), soma (oblation), *chandra* (moon), *virya* (virile essence), and bindu (the point that separates the nonmanifest from the manifest). Thus in the human being, the microcosm, the plan is contained in the male seed and only becomes reality through the matter that nourishes it in the mother's womb, in the egg, the point from which every living being has its origin.

SEXUAL UNION: *MAITHUNA*

Swami Karpatri tells us that "Those who do not acknowledge the divine nature of the linga, who do not understand the sacred character of the sexual rite, who consider the act of love vile and despicable, or as a mere physical function, are certain to fail in their attempts at material and spiritual realization. To ignore the sacred character of the linga is dangerous, whereas by worshipping it one obtains pleasure *(bhukti)* and liberation *(mukti)*."[11]

The *Chandogya Upanishad* compares the sexual act to sacred rites:

> The first appeal is the invocation of the god *(binkara)*. The invitation represents the hymn of praise *(prastara)*. Lying down close to the woman is the hymn of glory *(udgitha)*. Lying face to face is the choir *(pratihara)*. The orgasm is the consecration. Separation, the final hymn *(nidhana)*. Thus, the hymn to Shiva is woven out of the act

> of love. He who understands that this hymn is based on the sexual act recreates himself at every copulation. He lives long and becomes rich in progeny, cattle and renown.[12]

By dominating the sexual instinct, we can acquire physical and mental power. It is through sexual union that new beings come into existence. This union thus represents a link between two worlds, a point where nonbeing and being touch, where life is manifested, and where the divine spirit is incarnated.

The forms of the organs that accomplish this ritual are symbols. They are the visible form of the Creator. When Hindus worship the linga, they are not deifying a physical organ, but simply recognizing an eternal, divine form manifested in the microcosm. The phallus is the image of the divine emblem, the eternal, causal form of the linga, present in all things. The phallus is the godhead "that goes beyond the width of ten fingers."[13]

Transmission of the genetic code, its implantation in a rigorously chosen terrain, the transfer to a new being of the ancestral heritage comprising the archetypes that issued from the divine thought, is the most important religious act in a man's life. It must be considered as a rite and practiced according to very strict rules taking various facts into account, including astrological data, so that the new bearer of the torch is suited to his role and the species fashioned through a long series of ancestors continues without being debased or dying out on the way.

All religions, including Christianity, attribute a central ethical role to the procreative act, even if they have lost its meaning and inverted its values: the fault lies not in sexual amusement, but in mismatched fecundation.

The rites of procreation are carefully described in the *Tantras*. They include worship of the organs, the images of the divine principles that will unite to accomplish the miracle. Not seeing the image of the divine principle in the procreative organs and not worshipping them as such is the first step toward moral decay and the degradation of the species.

THE IMAGE

According to architectural treatises, Shiva's emblem, the linga, is divided into three parts. The lowest part is square, hidden in the pedestal. It represents Brahma, the maker, the power of gravitation that forms the worlds. The central section is octagonal and represents Vishnu, the centripetal force of concentration that gives rise to matter. The top section is cylindrical and represents Shiva, the centrifugal force of expansion, the bursting forth of form and matter. The linga is gripped by the yoni, the receptacle. "The Universal Mother is his altar. The linga itself is pure intelligence."[14]

In the temple, the linga is placed at the center of the tabernacle, a dark cubic chamber that is the *garbagriha,* the matrix of the temple. The axis of the erect phallus determines the axis of the tower, up to its peak, thus evoking the Linga of Light, the world axis.

Just as the temple roofs are covered with gold, the god's emblem also is sometimes fitted with a golden cap. This cap, known as *kavacha,* "the sheath," comprises certain symbolic elements of the god's anthropomorphic image: the three eyes, the crescent moon, the crown recalling his supreme royalty over all beings and all the other gods. The cap can be used to transform the naked linga into a linga with a face *(mukha linga),* meaning that the seed, the procreative force, when sexually stimulated, can be controlled, directed, and absorbed by the mental element.

The cap sometimes has five faces, making it a five-faced *(pancha mukha)* linga. The faces represent those aspects of the god that govern the directions of space and the zenith. The aspects of Shiva connected to the directions of space are: Tat Purusha (eastward); Aghora (southward); Vama Deva (westward) and Sadyojata (northward). Maha Deva, his transcendent aspect, faces the zenith. Tat Purusha represents nature and the earth element; Aghora intelligence, the ether element, and speech; Vama Deva, the notion of individuality, the fire element, and sight; Sadyojata, the water element and the penis.

THE SNAKE

A snake winds around the linga and touches the orifice with its forked tongue. Shiva wears a necklace of snakes. The snake is the image of latent, sleeping energy, the source of sexual and mental power coiled up at the base of the spine, which the yogi utilizes in his attempt to conquer the upper worlds during his inner journey. The snakes protect Shiva. He wears snakes as ornaments and as a sacred thread. According to the *Grihya Sutra*—the texts concerning domestic rites—domestic offerings should be made to Shiva in places where snakes are found.

Only Shiva the healer can control snakes: At the dawn of the ages, he was the only deity able to save the world by drinking the poison that the snake Vasuki spat into the ocean. The poison got jammed in the god's throat, leaving a blue mark on his neck.

THE LINGA BORN-OF-ITSELF: *SVAYAMBU*

Just as the god is everywhere incarnate in visible form, the linga itself is manifest throughout the world. Objects appear, evoking the form of the divine emblem. Thus, the "linga of ice" appeared in the Amarnath cavern, which thousands of pilgrims go to worship every year.

In the sacred waters of the River Narmada, in central India, pebbles known as *shalagrama* are found, which recall the form of the phallus. They are greatly sought after and are collected and worshipped by many Hindus. As the *Narada Pancharatra* tells us: "The god's seed fell on the earth's surface and filled the world. It is this seed that caused the appearance of all the lingas of Shiva found in the infernal world, on earth and in heaven."[15]

THE SEXUAL BODY: *LINGA SHARIRA*

The living being is but a transient moment of the permanent reality that is the species. Although insignificant individually, each living being is at the same time essential as a link, like the links of a chain. He or she is like a relay bearer of the Olympic torch, the conveyor of a model, a permanent code that is transmitted from one individual to another.

Life's main characteristic is its capacity to reproduce, continue, and transmit itself. It evolves through thousands of generations. Man is called *linga dhara,* the bearer or servant of his sexual organ. His personality is of no importance, except to the very limited extent by which he may add some elements to the code he has received and which he must transmit within the context of the species to which he belongs. He is merely a link, but whereas good links reinforce, bad links weaken the chain.

The transmittable permanent element, the code that defines the possibilities of development for each individual, for each link, is included in the seed that transmits it. It comes forth from man's sexual organ just as the universe issued forth from the linga, the divine phallus. According to the well-known treatise of Shaivite cosmology, the *Samkhya Karika:*

> The program, the sexual body, exists prior to the physical development of its bearer. It is composed of intellect and other subtle faculties. But it can only function if it becomes incarnate, even though it is independent of the body. It is characterized by a Dharma, a "goal to be accomplished," which it carries with it at the moment when it quits one body to take on another.
>
> To accomplish the goal assigned to it in creation, the sexual code, the *linga sharira,* incarnate by the power of nature *(pradhana),* acts like an actor playing one role after another.[16]

THE APPARITION OF THE LINGA

The *Shiva Purana* relates the following story about the linga:

> There is an immense cedar forest called Daruvana, where numerous hermits lived who were Shiva worshippers, meditating ceaselessly on the Creator of the world. Thrice every day they performed the rites for the god's worship and sang hymns to his glory. One day, when the hermits had gone off into the forest to seek sacred herbs used

in the rites, Shiva—in order to put their faith to test—manifested himself in a strange form. He appeared resplendent, entirely naked. His body was smeared with ash, with no other ornament. He stood there, holding his penis in his hand and began to give an exhibition of obscene acts. Shiva had come to this place to show his benevolence toward the forest-dwellers, his faithful followers.

The hermits' wives were initially frightened but, to their surprise, many felt attracted and approached the god. Some tried to embrace him, others seized his hands. They began to fight amongst themselves. At that moment, the sages returned. Seeing a nude man in such a shocking situation, they were scandalized and infuriated. Deceived by the power of illusion and blinded by their prejudice, they cried "What is going on? What does this mean?"

The naked sage made no reply. The hermits shouted terrible imprecations at the man-god. "You are behaving indecently. You have violated the rules of the Vedas. May your sexual organ fall to the ground!" As soon as they had pronounced these words, the penis of the divine envoy, Shiva with the splendid body, dropped to the ground. But it burned everything before it, wherever it went all was burned. It went down to hell; it climbed up to heaven; it ravaged the whole earth. Nothing was left anywhere.

All the worlds and all beings were in distress. The hermits were terrified. Neither gods nor sages would any longer know peace or joy. The gods and hermits who had been unable to recognize Shiva were consternated. They gathered together and went to the maker of the world, the god Brahma, to implore his protection. After singing his praise, they recounted to the god what had happened. Brahma said to them, "Brahmans! How is it possible that you, who are sages, could make such mistakes? How can you condemn poor ignorant beings for their faults if you behave just like them? Who among you can hope for peace again, after offending Shiva so badly? When someone refuses to honor an unforeseen guest who appears at the door at dinnertime, all merits acquired through the austerities are transferred to the visitor, who leaves as a heritage the burden of his crimes. What will then happen if the visitor is Shiva himself? Until the god's penis is stabilized, nothing good will come to the three worlds. That is the truth. The gods must do their utmost so that the great goddess, the daughter of the mountains, Parvati, will take the form of a vagina and grasp the divine phallus. Having taken the form of a vagina, Parvati must form the pedestal on which the phallus will be installed and worshipped with chants, perfumes, sandalwood, flowers, incense and offerings."[17]

LINGA WORSHIP

The *Linga Purana* teaches, "He who lets his life go by without having worshipped the linga is truly pitiable. If on one side of the scales we put phallus worship and on the other charity, fasting, pilgrimages, sacrifices, virtues, it is the adoration of the linga, source of pleasure and liberation which protects from adversity, that carries the day."[18]

"He who worships the linga knowing that it is the prime cause, the source of consciousness and the substance of the universe is closer to me than any other being."[19]

Why do we worship the linga? We worship it because it is the symbol of permanence, the archetype that reveals the nature of Universal Man, Purusha. Worshipping the linga means acknowledging the presence of the divine in what is human. It is the opposite of anthropomorphic monotheism that projects human individualism on to the divine world. In the instrument of procreation, we joyfully worship the Creator principle, since the procreative organ is also the instrument of pleasure, which, for a fleeting moment, gives us a glimpse of divine bliss. The divine state is made up of three elements, which are existence, consciousness, and sensual delight *(sat chit ananda)*. Only sensual delight belongs to the domain of experience. Through it therefore we have a foretaste; we can touch the divine state.

The linga cult implies worshipping the world's harmony and beauty, respect for the divine work, for the infinite variety of forms and beings in which the divine dream is manifested. It reminds us that each of us is merely an ephemeral being and of little importance, that our sole role is to improve the chain we represent for a moment in the evolution of our species and to transmit it. The phallus cult consequently involves recognition that the species is permanent compared to the impermanence of the individual, recognition of the principle that establishes the laws from which we derive and not their accidental or temporary applications, of the principle of life and not the living being, of the abstract and not the concrete. It has implications at all levels, whether ethics, the rites, cosmology, society, and so on.

Neglecting the linga cult in order to worship a person, whether divine or human, is a form of idolatry, an outrage to the Creator principle. It is the sin of pride, which seeks to reduce the divine to the image of the human. All the sacred texts of Shaivism—the *Puranas,* the *Tantras,* and the *Agamas*—repeat that only those that worship the divine phallus will be saved, that any society that abandons its cult and respect for the sexual body is doomed to failure and will be annihilated as were the Asuras, the race of humankind that preceded our own.

The Three Doors

According to the Samkhya, the transcendent Being who dreams up the world is forever unknowable. When this indefinable Being wishes to give its dream an appearance of reality, an emanation of its essence crosses the barrier between the nonexistent and the existing, the indivisible *(nishkala)* and the divisible *(sakala)*. At this point, the Creator principle appears, the origin of both world and beings. The latter are to be the witnesses, the spectators of the divine game *(lila)* that is creation, thus giving it an apparent reality. The divisible principle is formed of three inseparable components, the basis of all that exists. They form the substance of the Creator and of the created. These three components or doors are called existence *(sat),* consciousness *(chit),* and felicity *(ananda).*

From the point of view of existence (sat), for any created being, whether a star, an atom, or a living being, there are two crucial instants, known as "passages" *(dvara),* corresponding to those moments when nonexistence and existence touch each other, when the creator principle is in direct contact with the created being. These two passages through which a living being enters into contact with its Creator are birth and death. This is why the mother's womb and the funeral pyre are magical and sacred places. Ascetics venerate the reproductive organs and smear their bodies with the ash of the funeral pyres in their attempt to go closer *(samipya)* to the divine being.

The second door is consciousness (chit). Through knowledge, human beings seek to understand the nature of the world and the secret of its origin. This is the metaphysical way of Samkhya and its corollary Yoga, whose aim is to explore the interior universe of the human being, the image of the Universal Man, Purusha. It is also the way of asceticism, which—by controlling and mastering the body's impulses and energies—multiplies mental powers, making it possible to open the door of the sentient being onto the secret nature of the world, which the barriers of our senses prevent us perceiving.

The third door is sensual pleasure *(ananda)*. It is mainly at moments of sexual pleasure that we forget our human worries, our interests, and virtues, and rediscover that state of happiness and enjoyment that is part of the nature of the divine Being. In the act of love, we are most simply, most innocently close to the divine and, if we know how to become aware of it, and perceive directly the divine nature of sensual pleasure, here, too, we open the most direct and most immediate passage between the human and the divine. This is why mystics always express themselves in terms of physical love. It is not that vague glow of benevolence for all creatures, called "love" in a devalued sense, but the experience of intense happiness in which our being participates in the nature of the divine and, eventually, collaborates in the mystery of the creation of life.

Tantric rites and practices, open to all without any restriction of caste, gender, or nature, are meant to permit anyone to draw closer to the divine through these three passages, on the levels of existence, consciousness, and sensual pleasure. Tantric practices are many, because there is no aspect of the created, no form of action that is not an image, a reflection, an expression of the nature of the divine being. The substance of the world and of its Creator are one, and each of these multiple aspects bears the mark of the triple nature of the principle from which it has come forth.

Shaivism and Third Nature

With regard to male-female relationships, Shaivite mythology considers the world principle to be androgynous. The transcendent aspect of the divine is half-female *(ardhanari)*. The two aspects of the being separate so that the spark of sensual pleasure can appear between them, which is why their symbol is the linga, the erect phallus gripped by the vulva.

Although love is the aim of the separation of male and female principles, it is not necessarily tied to procreation. The god and the goddess engender children separately. Skanda, the god of beauty, leader of the heavenly armies, was born from the offering of Shiva's sperm into the mouth of the god Agni, the sacrificial fire. Ganesha, the guardian of doors, issued from the skin of the goddess alone.

The elementary forms of matter and life multiply by parthenogenesis or by mental projection. It was only later on in the order of creation that the uniting of the sexes was utilized as an incitement to and an instrument of procreation. Beneath the appearance of opposites, basic androgyny is always present and plays an important role in any search for the divine.

We find three genders in all things: masculine, feminine, and the undivided (or neuter). Texts on procreation rites, like the *Shiva Svarodaya,* explain how to give birth to a male, female, or neuter child. Grammar recognizes these three states or genders. The neutral gender is called nonmale *(napunsaka)*. In the human being, it covers all degrees of intersexuality. Nowadays this term is often translated as "eunuch," which is improper, because it is a question of nature and not of any surgical transformation, although ritual castration is not unknown among certain mystics, in India as in ancient Greece.

Every being is basically bisexual and the male-female ratio varies. In the context of the traditional castes of India, the warrior is feminine as compared to the priest, the merchant is feminine as compared to the warrior, and the peasant is feminine as compared to the merchant.

MOHINI, THE ENCHANTRESS

The bisexual nature of the divine is reflected in certain myths of India. The god Vishnu, who incarnates *sattva,* the force of world cohesion, is a masculine aspect of the goddess. He is feminine as compared to Shiva, who represents *tamas,* the original force of expansion. Vishnu is consequently often represented in an effeminate form. Sometimes he is even completely transformed into a woman and is called Mohini, the enchantress. In this guise, he undertakes to seduce Shiva, and a son is eventually born from their union. This son is the Tamil god Aiyanar Shasta, who is worshipped in the south of India. A similar story is told in one passage of the *Kanda Puranam* in the Tamil language:

> Vishnu, in the guise of the enchantress Mohini, went to repose near the ocean of milk. Shiva wished to show the world that Vishnu was merely one of his four wives. He drew near and manifested his desire to unite with him. The god tried to refuse, saying that a union between persons of the same sex was infertile. The Lord pointed out to him that he was only the personification of his Shakti, of one of his powers, and this was why he had been able to give birth to Brahma, the artisan-creator of the world, who came forth from his navel. And that he had, moreover, taken the form of a woman to seduce the hermits in the forest of Taruka, to distract them from their ascetic practices through which they were developing powers that threatened the supremacy of the gods.
>
> Since Vishnu remained stubborn, the Lord took him in his arms

> and bore him into the shade of a sal tree on the edge of the sea, to the north of the continent of the rose apple tree. There he united with him. The sap that they spread was transformed into a river, which took the name of Ganges. . . . From the union of the Lord's sperm with that of the dark-skinned god was born a child with a black body and red hair, carrying a bouquet in his hand. The three-eyed god (Shiva) named him the son of Shiva-Vishnu (Ariharaputtiran). He granted him several gifts . . . as well as sovereignty over one of the celestial worlds. When Ariharaputtiran appeared before Indra, the king of heaven, mounted on a white elephant and surrounded by the ganas, those delinquent adolescents who are Shiva's companions, the latter prostrated himself before him.[1]

This theme is also seen in the *Ramayana:* when the young hero god Rama was exiled to the forest, the hermits who lived there were so excited by his beauty that they forgot their spiritual exercises and sought physical contact with him. Rama politely refused, saying that in this life he had taken a vow of fidelity to Sita, his wife, but he promised them that, in their next existence, they would all be reborn as cowgirls and he, in the form of Krishna, would then satisfy their ardor.

HOMOSEXUALITY AND BISEXUALITY IN TRADITION

Because they evoke the primordial hermaphrodite, any sexually ambiguous being is of a sacred nature, whether they are physically or only instinctually intersexual. Every bisexual being can be considered as an emanation of the god's transcendent aspect. The hermaphrodite, the homosexual, and the transvestite thus have a symbolic value and are deemed to be privileged beings, images of the Ardhanarishvara. By virtue of this, they are considered to bring good luck and play a special role in magic and Tantric rites, as also in shamanism.

This magical aspect of intersexuality is found in all ancient civilizations. In ancient literature, groups of transvestite prostitutes, united around a guru, had an acknowledged place in society. Transvestite prostitutes are still found in most Indian villages where they are regarded with contempt as well as respect. In the popular theatre shows of Ramalila and Krishnalila, they are traditionally the ones who act the part of the goddesses and shepherdesses. The presence of a transvestite prostitute is still considered auspicious, particularly at a marriage ceremony.

Among shamans, divinatory powers are connected with bisexuality. "The final aim of Tantrism is to reunite the two polar principles Shiva and Shakti in our own bodies. . . . Initiatic androgyny is not always marked by an operation as among the Australians. In many cases, it is hinted at by dressing the boys as girls and vice-versa the girls as boys. . . . Homosexual practices, witnessed in various initiation ceremonies, can probably be explained by a similar belief, i.e., that the neophytes, during their initiatic instruction, embody both sexes."[2]

Divine androgyny can be evoked as a sadhana, a method of spiritual realization. Some mystics seek to unite with the god they worship by becoming a woman, dressing and living as such. This was the case, at the beginning of the twentieth century, of Ramakrishna, who founded a religious order that bears his name.

A great number of the wandering monks who transmit magic powers are recruited from among those marked with the seal of the hermaphrodite, who by nature are not inclined to procreation. Being outside the caste system, they act as a bond between the various levels of society. A companion-disciple, who is both lover and servant, often accompanies such monks.

As seen by Shaivism, homosexuality is a constant that can be observed in any society. It is part of the reality of the created world and is thus a manifestation of one aspect of the divine. Shiva's son, Skanda, is opposed to marriage and "has no other spouse than the army." He is the male deity worshipped by homosexuals and transvestites, who go in crowds on pilgrimage to his sanctuary.

In traditional society, sexual practices among young people—what is known as "schoolboy eroticism" (*langa dost* in Hindi)—are looked upon benevolently. Purification rites are practiced as after any sexual act. In the social ethics derived from Jainism, however, homosexuality is viewed as a deviance. This contrast continues in Indian society down to our own times. India is both the land of the *Kama Sutra,* of erotic temple sculptures, and of the most exacerbated puritanism. Recent invaders, the Muslims then the British, have considerably accentuated this latter aspect.

In modern society, despite that extreme puritanism displayed by the anglicized governing class, homosexual practices traditionally present no problem, except for persons with sacerdotal functions, who are ritually forbidden to practice oral sex. Furthermore, for everyone, purification rites are obligatory after any sexual act, which is something that foreigners do not always understand.

Insights into Initiation

The notion of initiation is based on the principle of counter-evolution, as clearly shown in Hindu tradition, according to which the first humans were sages, seers *(rishis)*, still very close to the Creator and the gods, endowed with vast knowledge, profound wisdom, and limitless powers. These sages transmitted their powers to their disciples and to their descendents from generation to generation. As the world degenerated through the four ages of humankind, from the Age of Gold or Truth (the Satya Yuga) to the Age of Conflicts in which we are now living (the Kali Yuga), transmission of powers and essential knowledge has inevitably become increasingly limited, and consequently more secret, since fewer and fewer persons are qualified to receive certain knowledge.

Initiation has thus been reserved for an elite, forming groups that seek to maintain islands of wisdom in the midst of a degenerating world and to preserve the elements of knowledge, which—after the catastrophes that will end the Kali Yuga—will be the seed of a new Golden Age. No prophet, no incarnation or envoy of the gods enters human society without receiving an initiation into this primordial tradition, considered as a second birth, of which Christian baptism is a symbolic remnant. Rama, the incarnation of Vishnu, was initiated by the sage Vishvamitra, while Jesus received his initiation from John the Baptist, an Essene.

The final aim of initiation is total realization of the human being on a spiritual level. This goal can only be reached in stages, successive steps. In every profession, in any walk of life, there are in principle degrees of initiation marked by rites of passage. In the modern world, these are sometimes fairly degenerate and symbolic, except in cases where an element of continuity, an unbroken chain of transmission, is maintained and where the rites maintain their properly initiatic character and validity.

In any society that still conforms to the preestablished cosmological order, different functions are distributed according to the aptitudes of the various human groups. Just as we have hunting dogs, guard dogs, and sheepdogs, there are also species of humans whose aptitudes fit them for the social roles of hunters, shepherds, laborers, warriors, or intellectuals. The final goal of all human existence is spiritual realization, but since the point of departure lies in the social order, each grouping has its own distinct initiatic rites, stages, and paths, according to caste or corporation.

The first stages of initiation are in some way selective, so that certain powers will only be transmitted to qualified individuals, to exclude their being mastered by persons who are not worthy or who are unsuitable. Many of the problems of the modern West derive from the fact that people without the essential qualifications and virtues required occupy key posts. With the rites of consecration, the kings of France received certain powers of healing that the presidents of the Republic do not possess, and such powers were an external sign of the validity (though relative) of their kingly initiation.

TYPES OF INITIATION

There are four main kinds of initiation: initiation as a craftsman, initiation as a king or warrior, priestly initiation, and spiritual initiation. In India, the last is most often connected to a certain form of monastic life. The monk's initiation represents what we may term "high" initiation, through which knowledge of a superior order is transmitted with its accompanying powers. Owing to their absolute value and independence from material civilization, these monks form the kernel into which tradition can retreat at times of disorder and crisis, without its existence being suspected or its custodians known. Curiously, caste status has nothing to do with this highest form of initiation, but only individual qualifications.

Initiation of Kings and Farmers

Initiation as a warrior (which is also that of the kings) presents fairly elaborate steps, since royal power plays a fundamental role in the stability of society. The farmer's initiation, on the other hand, is characterized by quite simple rites, essentially linked to the fertility of the soil. Any initiation includes tests to ensure that the recipient is worthy, since it requires the practice of certain virtues and the courage to bear considerable responsibilities connected with the powers transmitted.

The *Bhagavad Gita* deals with the hero Krishna recalling Prince Arjuna to his duties as a warrior. His initiation, received from Drona, a qualified master, requires him to be brave, to fight, even if it involves sacrificing his kin and risking his life. He has no right to withdraw into pseudo-monastic life, for which he is not qualified and which—for him—would represent cowardice, the abandoning of his duties.

Farming rites are highly important in prehistoric society, which we wrongly deem primitive; they tend to disappear in more complex societies. Such rites may include forms of cannibalism, to assimilate the virtues and strength of the person devoured, or sexual rites to ensure the fertility of the soil, as still encountered in Africa. Christian rogations to obtain rain, or the similar Inca rites still practiced in Peru, are remnants of traditional farming ceremonies. They require the presence of an initiated shaman and it would be a mistake to doubt their effectiveness a priori. I am sure that, returning to their true nature as human beings in the face of the disasters that threaten agriculture nowadays, many Westerners, who think that they are materialistic, would—if they knew them—still practice the rites to invoke Indra, the rain-god. Worship of the earth that nourishes us and the seasonal rites practiced in India are both connected to the traditions of farming populations.

Initiation as a Craftsman

For craftsmen, initiation rites vary according to the social role of their profession. By far the most important are those connected with architecture, because they are linked to the symbolic and magical aspects of building temples, the dwellings of the gods. A chief craftsman who is incapable or unaware of his responsibilities can draw down the gods' curse on the temple and on the kingdom. The architect or builder is also responsible for the correct design and construction of human dwellings, in which proportion and orientation play an essential role in ensuring that each part of the house is suited to a particular function, with a benevolent rather than malign influence on its inhabitants.

Since the architect is responsible for the magical value of the temple and the harmony of the home, admission into the builders' corporation is very strict, the degrees of initiation are many, and the rules difficult. Builders are required to gain a thorough knowledge of the symbols that convey the fundamental codes of creation. Every substance in the universe, all matter, and every shape can, in cosmological theory, be reduced to a ratio of forces expressed in turn by numerical ratios. In every aspect of the world, the Samkhya looks for certain constants representing the very principle of creation, which we may describe—to use a modern term—as the genetic codes used by the Creator to give birth to the world. If we manage to isolate some precise elements of these fundamental codes, we can perceive the intimate nature of all things, and also pass from one order of existence to another, since this basic data applies ineluctably to the perceptible world just as it does to those worlds that are invisible to us, to the intellectual sphere just as to the field of the senses, to the principles of vegetal or animal life as it does to the structures of matter.

It is these basic data that are called "the symbols." There is nothing arbitrary about real symbols. On the contrary, they are the expression of the deepest reality of all things. That is why the use of symbolic diagrams or formulas in the construction of temples ensures that they are places of real communication with the transcendent worlds, the exact representation of both the world of the living and of the heavenly worlds. Such diagrams, the geometric expressions of transcendent realities, serve as a basis for any architectural structure. In the case of temples, the diagrams differ according to the aspect of the deity whose presence is to be attracted there.

For homes, the diagram is schematized in human form, called *purusha*. The house can be oriented differently according to the profession of its occupants, and the various parts of the body of the purusha will determine which areas of the house are suited to sleeping, work, or study, for use as kitchens or bathrooms, for procreation or pleasure. The love chamber—the *rati mahal*—is usually on the first floor, which is not where the residents sleep. Furthermore, the proportion of the rooms and the openings is highly important and has a profound effect on the people living there. These symbolic rules are universal in character, and we find traces of them everywhere. They are transmitted through the craftsman's initiation to suit changes in religion or culture. Often, the master craftsman does not know their meaning, but he observes the tradition.

In sculpting the images of the gods, the craftsman traces on the stone the diagram corresponding to the characteristics of the divine aspect he envisages, then—while carefully observing its delimitations—he gradually releases from the stone the image that is hidden within. This is the opposite of the process used by Leonardo in his drawings to determine the proportions of a human body. In this case, the body is recreated according to the principles of its subtle nature. Erotic sculpture plays a very important role because the related diagram reconstructs in human form the complete being before its division. The supreme deity can be represented by the aspect of the perpetual copulation of Shiva and Shakti, or in the form of the Ardhanarishvara, the hermaphrodite, that aspect of Shiva that unites within itself the two complementary male-female principles, thus representing the primordial aspect of the divine.

At all times, the true craftsman must be aware of the importance of his role in society and the value of his role. On the day of worship of Sarasvati, the goddess of the sciences, the use of tools is forbidden, whether compass, hammer, book, or musical instrument. They are placed on an altar and venerated as vehicles of the goddess, with flowers, incense, and ritual offerings.

Sacerdotal Initiation

Sacerdotal initiation is the most widely known, because priests play an essential role in the ordinary ceremonies of all religions and all castes, whether baptisms, marriages, funerals, or temple services. It is the priest, who, through his rites and ceremonies, integrates human beings into the social order, thereby establishing a kind of correspondence between the divine plan and human society. The initiated priest possesses the power to invoke the real presence of the deities in the symbol, temple, or image, and then to liberate the supernatural force that he has captured.

Sacerdotal initiation takes place in various steps, each of which implies the acquisition of certain knowledge. Thus, the apprentice has to learn the sacred language and ritual formulas. These, however, remain a dead letter until he receives them orally from a master qualified to transmit them. In the Christian church, this is the case of the consecration formula. The magical transmutation of bread and wine into the flesh and blood of Christ only takes place if the mantra, the magic formula, has been transmitted orally, following a certain ritual and without interruption, by priests ordained in a chain originating from the Last Supper. The apparent meaning of a mantra has only secondary importance, just as it cannot be translated without losing its magical effect.

The Vedic mantras are lifeless, powerless, if oral transmission is interrupted. The only value of books is as a memorandum. The inner vision, the realization of the mantra's power is described as an extraordinary experience, like a lamp that ignites itself to illuminate everything around it.

Sacerdotal initiation comprises four stages. During the first, the child whose birth predestines him for this function receives a name and is thus incorporated into a particular tradition. A Hindu will not be called Mohammad, or a Muslim Krishna. It is a curious fact that in secular France, the town hall sometimes refuses to register babies with a Breton name, because that name is not included in the calendar of Christian saints. In actual fact, worship of the empire's gods is a fundamental element in the cohesion of any society, and some initiatic elements still exist in societies that claim to be most liberated.

The second sacerdotal initiation takes place when the boy is about twelve, on the threshold of adolescence, when he leaves the women's quarters. Called *yajnopavita* among the Hindus, its essential feature is the handing over of the sacred thread, considered as a second birth.

From this moment on, the boy is deemed sufficiently responsible to follow the strict rules of ritual purification and take part in the ordinary rites, particularly the puja, or ritual worship of the image or symbol of a god, the veneration of his master, of the sacred books and cult and work accessories. Thereafter and up to the end of his studies, the candidate for priesthood has to practice ritual purifications, serve his guru, and observe certain rules of life.

At the end of his studies, he receives initiation into the priesthood and a secret name. The magical mantras will be whispered into his ear in an isolated place, usually a forest or a riverbank, or a sacred pool, never in a house or temple, because the temple is for worshipping the god. The temple is the god's dwelling and not a place for practicing rites concerning human beings. That is why the public is not admitted to the sanctuary, just as they are not admitted to the king's apartments.

After the initiation ceremony giving him the power to perform the rites, the neophyte has to wear a yellow robe and take up the pilgrim's staff. He must visit the holy places while begging his food. The journey is at the same time an outer symbol of the inner journey the adept has to accomplish to achieve final realization. In practical terms, the journey is often reduced to a mere symbolic promenade. The symbolism of the journey *(safar)* is found among the Islamic Sufis, as a practice of detachment.

It is only after this pilgrimage that the priest's marriage ceremony can take place, arranged according to caste, degree of kinship, and the concordance of horoscopes, which will ensure fully the continuation of a sacerdotal dynasty. Thus the marriage of brahmans always takes place rather late, although the betrothal has been arranged much earlier, according to caste rules, with a girl whom the husband will see for the first time at their marriage ceremony. Brahmans are forbidden to have many children, since the caste must not be numerous.

India also has nonbrahman families of priests belonging to castes considered as workers *(shudras)*. These shudra priests are perfectly qualified for all temple rites and services. Their initiatic lineage goes back to the remotest periods of protohistory and comes from the Shaivite-Dionysiac religion. In fact, Shaivism is the origin of initiation and of the rites known as Tantric, which—according to this tradition—are the only ones that are really effective in the Kali Yuga, the age in which we are living. In the Vedic tradition, on the other hand, the god Shiva is accused of having revealed the secrets of initiation to the shudras, the humble, who do not belong to the "chosen" Aryan race. The two traditions continue to coexist everywhere in India. In some temples, like the Lingaraja at Bhuvaneshwar in particular, services are performed alternately by brahmans and by shudra priests.

It is only in the Shaivite tradition that persons born in civilizations that do not observe the rules of caste may be really assimilated and may have access to all degrees of initiation, if they prove that they have the necessary qualifications. In the Shaivite tradition alone can persons belonging to the craftsmen's castes or even born outside the sacred land of India have access to all degrees of initiation. This is so particularly for Westerners. Every one of us must seek to realize ourselves, based on the reality of what we are by birth, with the aptitudes, qualities, and status we possess. A black cannot become a white, nor a shudra become a brahman. Once we have fully realized our state of being, we can go beyond it and achieve further realizations, but we cannot change our category on a social level.

Traditional society is thus like a pyramid, in which the four faces (the four castes) only meet at the summit. Most Westerners who have sought to identify with Hinduism have failed because they did not wish to admit to the principle that, if they had had the necessary qualifications for being brahmans—that is, exercising the priesthood in Hindu society—they would have been born in India and not elsewhere. It is interesting to note that all the pseudo-Hindu sects that now abound in the West are Vaishnavite and devotional in character and can in no case lead to any real integration with the Hindu world, or to any true initiation.

Once married, a priest may exercise all his priestly and ritual functions and transmit initiation. He becomes a link in the initiatic line that starts from the sages of the earliest times, through which are transmitted the powers they received from the gods. Should any doubt arise as to the continuity of the initiatic tradition and consequently as to the validity of the rites, the god Vishnu, who ensures the world's continuity, becomes incarnate and reorders the tradition, utilizing any surviving elements. This is what is known as an avatar, a descent. Hindu tradition speaks of ten descents *(avatara)* and even mentions a *mleccha avatar*, an incarnation among the Western barbarians, who has occasionally been identified with the Master of Justice, or Jesus Christ.

Indeed, it is by direct intervention that initiatic rites can be transferred from one religion to another. It should be noted that sacerdotal initiation is Vaishnavite in character. Vishnu is the aspect of the divine that tends to preserve the world and ensure its continuation, whereas Shiva is not only its principle but also its destroyer, its liberator. The sacerdotal aspect of religion thus contains an element of obscurantism, the rules of conduct that protect society and its institutions. Churches are consequently conservative and not liberating. The search for knowledge, for liberation from the chains of existence, is part of the Shaivite initiation, which we may term "high" or "spiritual" initiation.

Monastic or Hermetic Initiation

In the four castes, initiation refers to the social person's participation in the cosmological rite, in the work of the Creator, in maintaining society, and improving human conditions as a whole on the spiritual level. Monastic initiation is quite another kind and is placed at a different level. Its aim is the full realization of the individual on the spiritual level, beyond all contingencies.

Monastic initiation can only be granted to people chosen to transmit the highest secrets of knowledge and of the final human destiny. They belong to no caste, no social circle. Their hierarchy is secret and at its head is that omniscient being, who has sometimes been called the King of the World. They only belong marginally to the society of humankind, in their public teachings and directives. It is only when the survival of traditional society is threatened that some of them may be delegated to take part in the action, "go down with the brahmans to the field of battle," as the law of Manu says.

When the King of England, India's legitimate suzerain, betrayed his treaties with the princes and gave up sovereignty in favor of a political party, there appeared in India persons clothed in the monastic dress, of astonishing intelligence and culture, who, within a few months, set up a traditionalist party, magazines, newspapers, and youth movements, which rose against Gandhi, Nehru, and the Indian Congress Party. Today they form a strong opposition, which, at the right time, will take power and reestablish the traditional order, if, however, humanity as a whole can still be saved from the catastrophe that looms.

When part of humankind is deemed to be heading for destruction, the hermetic tradition may close up within its shell and stay there unknown until a new humanity arises that is deserving of its message. Usually, in India, the bearers of esoteric tradition don the orange robe of the saddhus, the wandering monks, who have no family, no attachments, no fixed dwelling, nor material possessions. They mix with the crowds of pilgrims and begging monks, and it is difficult at first sight to recognize them. Their powers are immense, their knowledge incredible. They possess the gift of languages, and an extraordinary memory. They can quote, without the slightest error, any of the sacred texts, which, in India, form a vast literature. They can speak even with the most savage animals, which do not fear them, and come to lie down at their feet. It is their duty to teach, wherever they may be, the myths, the moral virtues, elementary wisdom, whatever will help consolidate traditional society. This has nothing to do with their true role, however, which is magical and mysterious. They can read minds and see the future. They know human destiny and do their best to aid a society that is racing to its destruction. They are the guardians of a secret treasure of knowledge for the future of humankind.

When world conditions demand and some form of action is required, qualified persons—while remaining in the world—may receive what we may term a virtual initiation, which cannot as a rule be transmitted, but which allows them to play an exceptional role in human society. Some of these mysterious "initiates," like Christian Rosenkreuz, or Nicolas Flamel, or even Rasputin, who have appeared at certain moments in the Western world, most probably belonged to this category.

No one knows the degrees and rites of monastic initiation, except so far as the very first stages are concerned, which are similar to the final initiation of brahmans, because those who are admitted to this path never turn back and if they halt on the way, their destiny can be frightful, since they risk falling into the maleficent circuits of counterinitiation.

CEREMONIES

Initiation consists of transmitting the powers, aptitudes, and—eventually—intuitive knowledge of an initiated human being whose own powers come from supernatural sources. We cannot exclude the possibility of direct initiation by a supernatural being, but it would appear to be contrary to the rules of initiative transmission and, in such a case, it is difficult to know whether the initiating power is beneficent or malevolent. Mystics fall into one category and certain magicians into the other, since the latters' powers may derive directly from maleficent powers. This fact has often reinforced popular confusion between initiates and magicians, inasmuch as both possess exceptional powers. The history of the Christian world is sadly filled with witch-hunts that have served as a pretext for attacking initiatic organizations, instigated by "black" magicians playing on public credulity.

It was indeed the forces of destruction, which, infiltrating among those who held material and religious powers, attacked the initiatic traditions, making the Christian world a spiritual desert without a force that can stop its course to destruction. Knowledge and power then fall into irresponsible hands. Only very recently, a similar phenomenon has appeared in India, and a major Western pseudo-initiatic society has played an important role in this field.

In any hierarchic society based on initiation—and consequently conforming to cosmic or divine order—no science or form of knowledge can be transmitted to anyone unworthy of it, anyone who does not shoulder the accompanying responsibilities. Democratic teaching of all kinds of knowledge, even the most dangerous, without taking into account the moral value of the apprentices, can only lead to disaster. Even now, we see the results of this kind of folly, since it is by the generalized spreading of profane science that the end of this cycle of humankind is being prepared.

In a traditional society, knowledge cannot be sold, thus teaching cannot be had for money, and science is not squandered in the market place. A brahman teaching at a university and receiving a salary for it is, on principle, excluded from his caste and from any future initiation. It is due to these rules that in India there is an extraordinary difference in level between the teaching of the traditional scholars and that of the universities. The teaching of the scholars attains an incomparably higher level, even on a strictly exoteric plane.

Apart from the teaching that accompanies the various stages, the degrees of initiation are transmitted in the form of secret ceremonies, from person to person. The related rites are, generally, quite simple, especially with regard to the first degrees of monastic initiation, whose aim is not social and concerns only the transmission of spiritual values.

The apprentice who has received advanced teaching and has shown himself worthy of it, who practices the ordinary rites and purifications faultlessly and has demonstrated his attachment to traditional values, is admitted to the first initiation, administered by an intermediary on the order of a full initiate. The intermediary has himself already received an advanced order of initiation. He becomes the apprentice's guru and is owed respect and obedience, since he is taking on a responsibility similar to that of physical paternity, yet even more serious because it is a spiritual paternity.

The day is chosen according to astrological findings, and the apprentice prepares himself by fasting. He must then shave his hair and all his body hair except his eyebrows and eyelashes. He then takes a ritual bath and puts on a new and seamless garment. He accompanies his guru to an isolated place and sits facing west or south in a yoga posture before his master, who thus faces him looking eastward or north, as the case may be. The guru lays his hands on the apprentice and pronounces certain mantras, after which he whispers into his ear the secret mantra by which the apprentice will contact the supernatural world, which will be the basis of the rites he will perform and which will protect him from evil. He also gives him his secret name, connected with the deity the apprentice prefers to worship. He gives him a cord, which he will wear around his waist, beneath his clothes. After this, the apprentice worships his guru like a god, with flowers, fruit, water, offerings, and incense (representing the five elements), which are the spheres of perception of the five senses.

Later, the Grand Master will give him a rosary of wild seeds with 108 beads, which he will wear around his neck and use to repeat—three times a day—the mantra he received at his initiation. He may henceforth attend some of the teachings that the Grand Master imparts to his followers.

In monastic initiation there is no public ceremony, whereas public rites often follow royal and sacerdotal initiations. In the initiation of craftsmen, the new apprentice or companion is received into the corporation with rites and tests that publicly affirm his new rank.

TANTRIC INITIATION

In dealing with initiation, we cannot ignore Tantric initiation, which utilizes elements of a sexual nature. In the Christian world, these have often been the cause or more often the pretext for persecuting initiatic groups, whether such rites were practiced or not. Associating the demoniac with the sexual is peculiar to the Christian world. This is probably due to the fact that Dionysian rites—in which direct contact with the supernatural world was sought through states of ecstasy involving the whole of the human being—continued to be the true religion of the ancient world, against which Christianity was attempting to assert itself. "Evil is whatever is pagan" wrote the Christian historian Orosius in the fifth century.

It is relatively easy to overthrow state religions and official cults by replacing the gods of the conquered with those of the conquerors, while maintaining the same rites, which is what imperial Rome did without any great shock in the countries it conquered. Christianity followed this practice in certain regions. Erotic-mystic rites, however, and their powerful effect on the participants, had either to be assimilated or violently rejected by the new religion. Assimilation is the only way to maintain the continuity of any true mystic experience. This was the case with Mahayana Buddhism, which assimilated Tantric Shaivism and its rites, and also with Islam, where Sufism represents an assimilation of ecstatic ceremonies and an erotic-mystic approach to the divine. The Sufi *zikhr* (rhythmic chanting) scarcely differs from the Greek *dithyramb* (wild ecstatic hymn to Dionysus), which corresponds to the Hindu *kirtana* (hymn of glory). In the UNESCO record collection, I have published a Syrian zikhr and a zikhr recorded in Yugoslavia, which are closely related to the Greek Dionysian rites.

Numerous sects did their utmost to maintain a Dionysian type initiatic tradition in the Christian world but were ferociously persecuted for political reasons, which have nothing to do with truly religious values. Organisms whose aims are purely spiritual are thus persecuted when civil and ecclesiastical authorities seek to establish their total hegemony over souls. The Catholic Church has played this sinister role throughout the ages, just as Nazism and Marxism have done in our own times. The pretext of erotic devil worship was one of the arms used to destroy initiatic traditions. In actual fact, some initiatic groups managed to maintain their spiritual traditions in spite of public authorities and the churches.

In India, Shaivism—of which the Dionysian religion is only the Western branch—resisted first Vedic then Buddhist puritanism and has regained its predominant place in modern Hinduism with its essential method, which is Yoga in all its forms. Yoga is the only method whose aim is to determine the subtle structures of the human being, to define the human being's latent powers and to perceive those aspects of the material and immaterial world that are inaccessible to the senses. Only Yoga can explain the raison d'être of the powers transmitted by initiation. A person's real body is the subtle body, in which the centers of consciousness and vital and spiritual energies are located very differently from those that appear in the physical body. In the effort of introspection, having reduced the mind's agitation to silence, the yogi descends to the deepest part of the self. It is in the region of the sexual organs that one attains pure knowledge, nonmanifest intellect, and becomes aware of the cosmic being, *hiranyagarbha,* the "egg of light." Tantric theory establishes a link between the inner organ, pure intellect, the world principle, and the outer organ, the procreative organ, the source of life; it considers all other vital sensory or mental functions as secondary.

The divine is manifest in the form of consciousness and life. Consciousness is never inert, or lifeless. In the microcosm, the transmission of life is equivalent to the creation of the cosmos. It is essentially a divine act. According to Tantric principles, a man is merely "the bearer of his phallus." His whole being is conditioned by this procreative purpose, since it is through a succession of living beings that life, consciousness, knowledge, and initiatic powers are transmitted. At the same time, since the divine state is a state of total well-being, it is in the instant of procreative pleasure that a person is closest to god and glimpses divine bliss. The divine state thus has as its image that spark of bliss that derives from the uniting of the procreative organs. Shiva is represented in the form of an erect phallus, in perpetual union with the female organ, an image of Shakti, the primordial energy from which the world came forth. The mother is a receptacle that receives the seed and from which the living being comes forth.

In Tantric theory, it is through practices of an erotic nature that the initiate can feed the energies needed for action, overcome all obstacles, and draw near to the divine. This is not merely through procreation alone, but through the illuminating nature of pleasure. Any sexual act can be organized as a magic rite. It is at the moment of sexual union that we can in some way couple up to the divine, since, according to the *Chandogya Upanishad,* the enlightening nature of pleasure can become the starting point for true experience of the divine state.

The energy coiled up at the base of the spine can then mount through the various centers of the subtle body, wakening all one's latent powers, and reaches the open door at the top of the skull through which the adept can leave the material body and unite with the divine. Such experience, which demands from the very start the suppression of all the mind's agitation, is both difficult and dangerous, requiring a reliable guide and rigorous initiatic discipline. The degrees of Tantric initiation are complex and its rites extremely secret.

According to the *Tantras,* there are two ways to spiritual and mystic realization: the right-hand way, which utilizes the energy diffused in the human being, and the left-hand way, which finds its direct support in procreative energy and utilizes transfigured sexual experience. The latter is the quickest and most effective way, but most dangerous, since the powers it unleashes can become insurmountable obstacles if one stops. It is thus that magicians are created, being in fact fallen adepts.

It is very important to know Tantric initiation, since all groups seeking mystical experience utilize the language and the symbols of love, even if in practice Tantric ritual is excluded. Tantric rites are of two kinds, according to whether the predominant aspect is the female principle, or Shakti, in which the female organ is worshipped as the primordial cave whence the human race came forth, or Shaivite rites, in which the phallus is worshipped as the source of life.

In the final analysis it seems that all initiation is ultimately connected with Shaivism, or with its kindred Dionysian or Sufi forms. Traces of such an origin can be detected in authentic initiatic groups in the Christian, Vedic, Taoist, Buddhist, and Islamic worlds.

The transmission of certain initiatic powers is independent of the value of the individual. The initiatic seed, like the seed of life, can be transmitted through many insignificant generations and regains its bloom at the right moment. Naturally, the tests the neophyte undergoes aim at selecting worthy candidates. One must be careful, however, in seeking to judge an initiatic tradition by some of its representatives, who may be merely its vehicles, or who may have only an apparent role, serving to mask the true holders of initiatic power.

In view of the rise of materialism and the aberrant, irresponsible, and inhuman egalitarian theories that are a feature of the Kali Yuga, announcing the destruction of the greatest part of humankind, only initiatic societies can keep alive that spark of spiritual life and transmit those essential truths that will allow some of humanity to survive the catastrophe. They represent the soul of the social body. Whether Hindu, Buddhist, Islamic, or Christian, such authentic initiatic societies are the only ones that practice the methods by which we can reconquer wisdom, draw near to the divine, and realize our transcendent nature.

The Science of Dreams

Dreams—why they occur and their meaning—have always been a subject of wonder and curiosity. The prophetic value of certain dreams has been the subject of speculation and attempted interpretation in all civilizations. In India, the theory of dreams and search for their meaning appear in various works under the general heading of *Svapna Vichara* (the interpretation of dreams).

Dreams are of various kinds. Their nature can be analyzed in relation to theories about the *siddhis,* the subtle powers belonging to the structure of living beings, which usually remain latent in the unconscious. Dreams take shape as the formulation of logical thought, based on innumerable data stored in our memory, which our thought mechanism keeps ceaselessly in movement. This inner element may be accompanied by external elements, which may be extrasensory perceptions, beyond the limits of time and space, or the intrusion of an external thought coming from living or subtle beings. The various elements making up the oneiric process must consequently be distinguished and the various kinds of dream considered separately.

ANCESTRAL MEMORY: *JATI SMARANA*

Certain elements of our genetic memory are connected to the transmission of life. It is on this basis that the fetus dreams that it is moving, walking, or feeding. At birth, the living being is ready for action. A chick, breaking out of the eggshell, already knows how it must behave.

The human baby works by starts and fits for a long time, incapable of utilizing the knowledge contained in its genes. Some elements in our genetic memory may survive from a very distant past: experiences, situations, visions, and characters that have impressed one of the ancestors of our lineage. This is *jati smarana,* our ancestral memory.

EXTRASENSORY POWERS: *SIDDHI*

According to Yoga theory, our powers of perception are much wider than the limitations of our senses. Yoga practices allow us to overcome these limitations, which also disappear in the state of sleep. Some of these powers allow us to perceive far-off objects and places. This visionary power is called *drikshakti.* We can also take part in events far from us in time—whether past or future—thanks to the power known as *prakamya* (transfer). Thus, in a dream we may perceive an accident or a death taking place on another continent, or take part in some past or future event in a place we have never seen. We may also be present at an event that has not yet taken place. Such powers form part of our "internal organ" *(antahkarana),* or "transmigrant body" *(linga sharira),* according to Yoga definitions. These are our psychomental structures and remain latent. As a rule they are not accessible in a waking state, unless we manage to control them through Yogic introspection. They also contribute a vast amount of material to the formation of our dreams.

THOUGHT COMMUNICATION

Another of the siddhis is thought communication, a frequent phenomenon and easily practiced. Sometimes we perceive a shock, a call, or a drama concerning someone close to us, by means of some kind of mental radio wave.

INSPIRED OR PROPHETIC DREAMS

Yoga also teaches a technique that allows our vital energy to penetrate another person, and even to reanimate the dead. By a similar process, a spirit, or subtle being, can take possession of a living being and speak through his mouth. Thus magicians, as well as subtle beings (spirits or gods), express themselves through the mouth of a medium in trance. This also happens in the case of prophets. The phenomenon is equally found in the form of prophetic dreams. In dreams, our guardian angel or a benevolent deity can warn us of dangers that loom and tell us how to avoid them.

Since logical thought is suspended during the state of sleep, the various sources from which a dream can draw its material are difficult to differentiate. Works on the interpretation of dreams—as numerous in India as elsewhere—seek to establish their characteristics, the presence of certain symbolic elements that make it possible to determine the character and nature of a particular dream. The different elements that come together to form a dream are, however, essentially personal and contingent. Although there is no doubt as to the existence of prophetic dreams, their sources and components are different in each case.

Poetry and Metaphysics

Although most *mantras*—verbal formulas enabling communication with the invisible—are monosyllabic, some are not. These longer mantras are based on *chandas,* poetic meters, which correspond to *talas,* the rhythmic formulas of music. Vedic texts are mentioned as *chandas,* underlining their magical and sacred power.

THE SACRED METERS

According to their numerical characteristics, meters correspond to the *yantras,* geometric formulas of magic diagrams, as well as to the harmonic ratios of *ragas* (musical modes) and talas (rhythms). Repeating them leads to the attainment of an ecstatic state and evokes the nature and presence of supernatural beings. All rites are based on a *chanda-yantra-mudra* (word-diagram-gesture) combination.

In sacred poetry, esoteric knowledge is transmitted through the chandas. The apparent meaning of the words is not necessarily their true meaning, which remains secret. The essence of poetry—whether sacred or profane—lies in its ambiguity, in its multiplicity of meanings. Each verse of the Vedas has thirty-two different meanings, applied to the various forms of knowledge, the sciences, and the arts.

Besides magic formulas themselves, which have no apparent meaning, all traditional knowledge is transmitted through chandas, that is, in versified form, ensuring the oral transmission of sacred texts, even through individuals who do not understand their meaning. This is true of all traditions that have preserved the magical character of esoteric transmission. Their versified form guarantees the permanence of the formulas and texts and avoids any distortion.

PSALMODY

According to Hindu grammarians, all languages were originally tonal. The chandas' metric elements possess an inseparable melodic content. Psalmody is an essential aspect of the transmission and power of sacred texts. In all civilizations belonging to the oral tradition, bards—who are in some way living books, and thereby possess magic powers—chant poetry.

Sacred poetry is thus a privileged tool for contacting the supernatural and transmitting esoteric knowledge. Chanda structures, which are parallel to those of the yantras and *svaras* (musical notes), reflect cosmic order and facilitate communication between different states of being. Rites do not exist without sacred formulas, without magical texts versified according to the rules of poetic meter.

MYSTICAL POETRY

At the same time, certain periods see the rise of mystical poetry, in which the apparent meaning predominates. This kind of poetry, connected to bhakti (devotion), helps those that sing it enter into states of mystical exaltation. It is, however, an already degenerate form of poetry, connected with religiosity. In no case can it be considered as having any metaphysical aspect, and it only flourishes in forms of religion that are the refuge of those in distress during the Kali Yuga.

SECULAR POETRY

This form of poetry has in turn given birth to secular and erotic poetry, which, as the Greeks noted, comes from the dithyramb. In India, too, the origin of the theater lies in the *kirtana,* the chanted narrations of the bards recounting the adventures of the gods.

Every inspired poet can instinctively find certain essential meters, as well as that poetic ambiguity that gives a universal value to the expressed meaning. In the modern world, poetry often finds its evocative force only when sung. The harmony of the svaras provides it with a dimension that is otherwise lacking.

The Cock

It seems to me that many modern works on ethnology and the history of religions rather neglect the interpenetration of cultures and ancient sources. For example, they rarely mention the way in which Cretan Dionysism—which was the religion of the Mediterranean world prior to the Dorian invasions—profoundly influenced Greek and Roman religion and, through them, the Christian world. It has left its traces everywhere in the popular religion of the Western world.

Many of the rites, beliefs, and symbols of Cretan Dionysism were closely related to those of pre-Aryan Shaivism in India. Such is the case of bull worship and sacrifice—the bull being Shiva's vehicle—found in Cretan, Greek, and Mithraic rites, and still existing today in the Spanish *corrida*.

In Shaivism the cock is the vehicle of Skanda, the virgin god of beauty and war, who came forth from Shiva's phallus, without any participation of the goddess. Skanda means the "spurt of semen." Having fallen into the mouth of Agni (the sacrificial fire) and thence into the sacred waters of the Ganges, Skanda was raised by the Pleiades. Skanda, whose cult is forbidden to women, is also known as "the adolescent" (Murugan in Dravidian, Kumara in Sanskrit, Kuros in Crete). In Sanskrit he is also Shanmukham (of the six faces), corresponding to the Sumerian Sumugan. The temples of medieval India contain innumerable images of Skanda, the leader of the gods' army, with his cock.

The familiar European representation of a cock on top of a belfry—the phallic symbolism and warrior nature of which have often been noted—

bears a rather curious analogy to the symbolism of Skanda. It bears witness to parallels between Shaivism and survivals of Dionysiac traditions in popular religion, in spite of Christianity.

Its representation also recalls probable relations, starting from the tenth century, between the guilds of Hindu architects and European cathedral builders, whose plans, orientation, and proportions are based on the same diagrams as the temples of India. The appearance of the bell tower, unknown in earlier temples, also recalls such an influence. Masonic associations, too, have preserved rites and symbols identical to those of the Hindu guilds. The Celts preserved the bull cult: why not that of the cock?

The Nature of Beauty According to the Samkhya

The notion of beauty is one of the most ambiguous and difficult to define. The word is employed to describe the harmony of a landscape, the quality of light, the perfection of a certain type of animal, the nobility of a symphony, the (erotic) attraction of a human being, or the perfection of a piece of architecture. The artists of ancient Greece and of the Italian Renaissance often sought to establish the ideal proportions of the human body for architectural purposes, but these did not necessarily lead to a general theory of beauty. Plato's definition "adaptation to custom" is merely an evasion, an avowal of ignorance.

For Shaivite cosmogony, the harmony of proportions, based on numerical ratios, is the secret of both material and living structures. Whatever exists is based on geometric elements, that is, numerical ratios. It is the diversity of harmonies—of proportional ratios—that gives rise to the various sorts of beings and constitutes their beauty. The world's nature is harmony, and the Creator's design is expressed in its beauty. It is by perceiving this beauty that we have some intuition of the secret of creation and the nature of the divine.

In order to evoke the origin and nature of the world, the Creator-god is symbolically represented as a dancer who, by means of the variety of rhythms and gestures of his dance—the *tandava*—gives birth to all sorts of beings, minerals, gods, trees, animals, and men, while the goddess, his companion, by the seduction of her more graceful dance—the *lasya*—causes female beings to appear.

YANTRAS AND RAGAS

Each species of living being, just like each mineral substance, comes forth from a code, a formula that becomes more and more complex as the varied forms of nature develop. To begin with, such formulas are simple, facilitating the classification of relationships among various forms of existence. There are analogies between certain subtle beings and minerals, plants, animals, and human types.

These simple formulas, sources of life and creation, are not merely abstract entities but active principles. At the origin of each line, we can conceive of an active genetic principle, a manifestation of divine thought in creation, a spirit or deity. These principles can be translated into various images, such as anthropomorphic, zoomorphic, or vegetal representations.

Shaivite cosmology seeks to summarize nature in the form of geometric diagrams, codes of proportions linked to certain key numbers. Such diagrams are called yantras. When Einstein suggested that, "in the universe, all is geometry," he was enunciating a principle that Indian cosmology has always held.

The system of the yantras, the magical diagrams evoking certain component principles of the universe, also allows us to establish some kind of communication with active powers—the gods they represent—rather like a telephone number putting us into contact with an invisible responder. The numerical-geometric elements evoking active subtle entities at all levels of existence are also found in the microcosm, in the human being, and we can analyze the emotional impact they have on the individual consciousness, since the raison d'être of our perceptions is to make us witnesses of the divine work. A world that is not perceived does not exist. Our senses are the mirrors through which the Creator's dream becomes reality.

YANTRA ELEMENTS

In static form, the yantras express the basic principles encountered at all levels of existence, life, perception, and thought. With their help we can, in some cases, discover how our emotive perceptions correspond to certain basic geometric and numerical factors, and on this basis an aesthetic theory can be established.

Some of the geometric elements utilized in the yantras are:

The fire triangle, pointing upward, which evokes the principle of expansion—ascendant and centrifugal—considered as male, whose equivalent is the phallus symbol. Fire tends to rise, to move outward from the terrestrial center of attraction. It symbolizes detachment, the mystic approach, tension, development, inequality.

The water triangle, pointing downward, evokes the principle of attraction—centripetal—considered as female. Water tends to find a horizontal equilibrium, to level out, and the water triangle represents attachment, the religious approach, appeasement.

In the symbolism of numbers, the fire triangle corresponds to the factors 3 (triangle) over 2 (base), while the water triangle corresponds to the factors 2/3. In music, the 3/2 ratio of the fire triangle corresponds to the frequency ratio of what we call "a fifth" (Do/So), an interval that to us appears as radiant, active, and glorious, whereas the 2/3 ratio of the water triangle corresponds to what is called "a fourth" (Do/Fa), which is a soft, passive, feminine interval. In music, multiples of the factor 2, which is neuter, correspond to differences of an octave and do not change the significance of the ratios.

When the male and female triangles touch, a spark occurs and the energy principle appears. This is represented by the figure symbolized by the "hourglass" shaped drum of the god Shiva.

When the triangles interpenetrate, creation takes place. The appearance of matter is due to the principle of gravitation, which gives birth to atoms and solar systems. It is represented by the star hexagon, which in music corresponds to movement, the series of fifths and fourths, giving rise to two basic hexagonal scales:

> C, D 9/8 = $2^2/2^3$, E + 81/64 = $3^4/2^6$, G 3/2, A + 27/16 = $3^3/2^4$, B + 243/128 = $3^5/2^7$
>
> C, B flat 8/9 = $2^3/3^2$, A flat 64/81 = $2^6/3^4$, F 2/3, E flat 16/27 = $2^4/3^3$, D flat 128/243 = $2^7/3^5$

Together, they form the twelve basic sound divisions of the octave used in all music. There is nothing arbitrary in this division. It merely indicates our aptitude to recognize certain numerical ratios directly by listening, just as we perceive visual ones.

The three basic elements of the world structure are called *tamas* (centrifugal force), *sattva* (centripetal force), and *rajas* (their resultant, which gives rise to gravitation, vibration, and rhythm). In one form or other, they are found at the basis of every aspect of the world. These three factors have been compared to a car battery or the connection between a positive (tamas) and negative (sattva) pole that produces energy (rajas), which makes the starter work.

In religious symbolism, these three principles are represented by an indivisible trinity, the source of the formation of worlds, with the aspect of the three gods: Shiva (tamas), Vishnu (sattva), and Brahma (rajas). Brahma is the craftsman, the artisan of the universe. Everywhere we find the star hexagon and the circle, born from its movement.

THE FACTOR OF LIFE

The formation of vibratory waves or rotation waves causes the appearance of a coordinate of space, which is time. A sound wave represents a given number of vibrations during a period of time. Time in itself, however, knows no absolute measurement, any more than space does. They merely represent relative values. The dimensions of space and time exist only in relation to a perception, to a consciousness connected to what we call life. A universe is not in itself any larger than an atom. Dimensions appear large or small in relation to the rhythm that serves as the basis of our perceptions.

According to Hindu cosmology, a form of consciousness or perception is present everywhere in the universe, in molecules, solar systems, and galaxies. It is manifest in the order of creation by the appearance of a new factor, the numerical factor 5, in the structure of molecules, star cells, and living beings.

Our perception of the dimension of space and time depends on the factor 5. Since life, feeling, and perception began, they have been linked to combinations of molecules in which the factor 5 plays an essential role. An ice crystal forming on a windowpane has six branches, but it is not alive. A starfish has ten: it lives, perceives, and acts.

The leaves of trees have five follicles, just as our hand has five fingers. We possess five senses. All structures of life and perception are linked to this magic factor, which is represented in the yantra system by the star pentagon, symbol of the god Shiva as the source of life, knowledge, and perception. In iconography, it is also evoked by the moon of the fifth day. This symbol is encountered in all religions.

The properties of the pentagon give life and emotion to architectural forms, hence the importance of the golden segment in the architecture of our ancient cathedrals. The golden segment is the ratio of the length of a diagonal drawn between two nonadjacent points of a pentagon and the length of a side. It corresponds approximately to the ratio of 1:1.62.

Even in our own times, an old Italian mason whom I asked to widen a window replied, "I can't do it, because it wouldn't be tall enough." A window that is one meter wide should be 1.62 meters tall, meaning the ratio of the golden segment. It is owing to the observance of these proportions that ancient Italian hovels have such an apparently inexplicable charm. It is the utilization of the golden number that lends harmony to Greek temples, and a mysterious charm to ancient cathedrals.

THE FACTOR 5 IN MUSIC

Music plays a major role in understanding the basic principles encountered at all levels of existence, life, perception, and thought—as the Greeks, following the Indians, remarked—since in music we can analyze the connection between frequency ratios, between sound waves and emotive factors. Musical modes make it possible to analyze our emotional mechanisms, and their relation with the numerical factors that determine them, just as they determine all our aesthetic perceptions. This is why music is considered as a kind of key to the arts and sciences.

Indian music has hundreds of modes, or ragas, that awaken the most diverse feelings. The word *raga* means "what moves, charms, pleases, attracts." Some sound ratios sound gay to us, while others stir up melancholy; trumpets make us think of war, and chants make us mystical. Even in such a rudimentary and artificial system as that of Western music, we feel the difference in the emotional climate of major and minor modes.

The intervals we find moving, sad, or tender, violent or aggressive, correspond to the factor 5. It is much easier to analyze them in modal music, built around a relation to a fixed tone, the tonic, as in Indian, Arabic, and ancient Greek music, rather than in Western music, which uses modulation (constant changes of the tonic) and in which the scale is distorted by the tempering of fixed-tone instruments like the piano.

Intervals can, however, be observed in expressive moments when voice, chords, and breathing abandon the tempered system. When an inspired performer suddenly plays a B flat that grips us and makes us shiver with emotion, he is using the same sound ratios as an Indian musician.

The main intervals featuring the factor 5 form two sets parallel to those of the triple system, the cycle of fifths. They are:

A $5/3$, E $5/4 = 5/2^2$, B $15/8 = 5 \times 3/2^3$, F sharp $45/32 = 5 \times 3^2/2^5$, D flat $135/128 = 5 \times 3^3/2^7$

B flat + $9/5 = 3^2/5$, E flat + $6/5 = 3 \times 2/5$, A flat + $8/5 = 2^3/5$, D flat + $16/15 = 2^4/5 \times 3$, F sharp + $64/45 = 2^6/5 \times 3^2$, B + $256/135 = 2^8/5 \times 3^3$.

The notes of the first set evoke feelings of sweetness, tenderness, calmness, melancholy. Those of the second are hard, enterprising, aggressive.

By uniting all these intervals, we obtain an irregular division of the octave into twenty-four intervals (in practice twenty-two), giving different nuances of expression for certain notes that the Indians call *shruti* ("what the ear distinguishes clearly"), since they form our total musical vocabulary.

Theoreticians of Indian music have carefully studied the psychological impact of these various intervals, thus making it possible—by combining them in different scales—to create the emotional climates of ragas. A parallel system exists for the color spectrum, the visible part of which corresponds to a musical octave, going from simple to double frequencies. These observations, together with those deriving from the yantras' geometric diagrams, have led to a general theory of aesthetics, that is, a code of proportions giving a coherent definition of what we call beauty, which is produced by a multitude of precise harmonies. There are hundreds of ragas, just as there are hundreds of types of beauty.

It is on these bases that canons have been established, definitions of proportion that are used as the basis for Indian sculpture.[1] Codes of proportions defining different kinds of beauty follow different canons. These canons cover all details, not only the proportions of the body, but of the face, the spacing of the eyes, the relative length of legs and arms, determining proportions that correspond to beneficent or maleficent beings, erotic or heroic.

Beauty is made of harmony, ugliness of discord. In both animals and humankind, genetic selection tends to establish the perfection of each type, explaining why a pedigree dog is beautiful and a mongrel is not. Each species of living being is born of a harmony, a code. Left to itself, nature improves and perfects each type, leading to extraordinary beauty in insects, flowers, animals, and humans. The principle of harmony and beauty is thus both the origin and outcome of creation, the raison d'être of existence. It is through harmony that we can apprehend something of the secret nature of the world and of the divine.

Music: The Language of the Gods

In Shaivite philosophy, as also in Pythagorean theory, music is considered as a kind of key to the sciences, as well as a means of communication between different states of being, between the human and the supernatural. It is the language of the gods. This is no arbitrary attribution, any more than is—to the popular mind—the representation of the world as being created by the rhythm of Shiva's drum. For Hindu cosmology, matter as such does not exist. The universe is formed only by relations of energy elements, tensions, vibrations, and movements.

Even the dimension of time only exists in relation to wavelengths, vibratory rhythms whose duration we perceive through a kind of clock within ourselves, which is nowadays termed the brain's alpha rhythm. The appearance of the world is due to the limitations of our senses. It would appear completely different to beings possessing other senses operating within other limits.

The phenomena of life, feeling, perception, consciousness, and thought all derive from the same formulas that are the basis for the formation of matter. This is why communication is possible.

There is thus a fundamental bond, or coordination, between matter and perception, which exist only for each other and through each other. Rare are the domains where parallelism—the linkage between the physical, mental, sensorial, and emotional—is easily discernible and can be traced back to comparable data or common formulas. Music is the most obvious example. The ratios of sound vibrations, which can be reduced to simple numerical ratios, are perceived as emotive stimulants, as means of psychological manipulation. They evoke images, create an aesthetic feeling, an emotion, establish a kind of communication between spheres that seem to be totally different, and even between different forms of being.

Thanks to this ubiquity, sounds, organized in a musical *(nada)* or verbal *(shabda)* form, can guide us in seeking those formulas of a more general kind that lie at the very foundation of creation as a whole, at the origin of all forms of matter and life. It is by utilizing these formulas in a rhythmic form that Shiva dances creation, thus giving birth to different forms of being. By virtue of the existence of these archetypes, of these formulas common to all aspects of creation, music allows us to evoke one order of existence within another, to communicate with spirits and gods.

MODERN WESTERN MUSIC

The mechanisms of our perceptions are of a proportional nature. They are not connected to dimension: A square is a square, whether it is large or small. All aesthetics are based on proportions, and the same is true of music. This is why the tempered piano, which claims to replace a proportional system with an additive system, by equalizing—that is, mutilating—the intervals, by replacing harmonic ratios with a division based on logarithms, is an aesthetic and psychological aberration.

This system has singularly oriented the development of Western music for more than two centuries and has made it very difficult to study the musical phenomenon as a whole. For example, studying various kinds of Oriental or ethnic music while utilizing as a system of measurement the hundredths of tempered semitones is aberrant, since it completely masks the proportional ratios that are the basis of all music and alone make it possible to explain its magical action.

The modification—or let us say sterilization—of intervals in the tempered scale deprives most Western music of its cosmic and psychological correspondence. Its logical result is a musically neutral structure, without any defined center, leading music to abstract forms stripped of any meaning or emotive impact. Such music is far from any universal reality and its only attraction lies in the extent to which it betrays its own principles, where something real can be glimpsed through its approximations. Xenakis's wife said of him one day, "Despite his theories, Yannis is a musician all the same." Such a remark could easily apply to the most important modern composers.

FACTORS 2, 3, AND 5

The real substance of music—sound material formed by a set of sounds utilizable and utilized in all music—is founded on harmonic progressions using the factors 2, 3, and 5 as a basis. If we study the basic structures of matter and the principles of life, we find the same numerical factors as in music. This is precisely why one can have an impact on the other.

From the point of view of human perception, the discernible intervals taken as a whole and having a precise significance within an octave (including the base sound and its octave) number fifty-four, sounds deriving from different combinations of the factors 2, 3, and 5 within certain limitations. These fifty-four sounds form the vocabulary of all music.

Hindu semanticists, such as Nandikeshvara and Bhartrihari, explain that the other form of sound language—spoken language—is also formed of fifty-four possibilities of articulation, which we call vowels and consonants, serving as the basis of all the world's languages. Any expression, any communication through the intermediary of sound, employs these 108 elements that are a constant in our perceptive mechanisms, our powers of mental classification, of cognition. This is why the figure 108, representing the sum of fifty-four musical sounds and fifty-four articulated sounds, is deemed sacred, as a symbol of the Creator-Word.

THE ACTIONS OF RHYTHMIC DIVISIONS

Rhythmic divisions and their psychophysiological action are based on factors similar to harmonic divisions. There is no difference in the nature of what we perceive as the pitch of a sound or its rhythms. Below sixteen vibrations per second, we perceive sound frequencies as beats. We are capable of coordinating these beats in rhythmic frames corresponding to harmonic frames. Psychophysiological reactions are the same.

Measures in 2, 4, 8, or 16 beat cycle form the framework of rhythmic developments and correspond to the octaves of the melodic scale. Rhythmic elements in 3 beat cycle create movement. Rhythms in 5 beat cycle cause emotive reactions and are consequently much employed in music intended to produce a psychological effect, as well as in ceremonies and dances of an ecstatic or magical nature.

In forms of music producing a psychological or cosmological action, extreme precision is required in the intervals and rhythms for them to be effective. Additional processes, however, such as differences in volume, touch, color, or metric or rhythmic nuances, can sometimes make up for any deficiency in pitch ratios, as in the case of piano music or the music of Indonesian gamelans. At the same time, rhythmic inaccuracy eliminates most of the music's physiological impact, so that it no longer induces an ecstatic condition, and no longer serves as a means of communication with the supernatural.

THREE ASPECTS OF MUSIC

For human beings, music has three main aspects: a ritual or magical aspect, a cosmological aspect, and a psychological aspect. These three aspects are sometimes mixed together and confused, whereas basically they are fundamentally distinct.

Magical Aspects

The purpose of what may be termed ritual or magical music is to establish communication with the invisible, with the transcendent forces that govern the world, with cosmic principles, the mysterious world of gods and spirits. Such forms of music are the basis of any ecstatic rite, any magical practice. There is no rite that does not involve some sound element.

Although in actual fact all music constructed according to the natural laws of acoustics and hearing possesses magical potential and ritual aspects, some sound forms serve solely for communication with the invisible.

Thanks to the parallelisms between certain musical formulas and those on which the structures of matter and life are based, it is possible to evoke the subtle beings, which we call spirits and gods, and let them manifest themselves and act. Ecstatic dances are a means of establishing contacts with supernatural forces that can then express themselves through the mouth of the dancer, who appears to be possessed by a spirit. This is what happens in possession dances and in ancient practices of a Dionysian kind, which can still be observed easily in the zikhr of the Middle East and the dances of African witch doctors. Such dances utilize repetitive rhythmic formulas that create a state of semiconsciousness. Sudden breaks in the rhythm then cause a psychological shock leading to a state of trance in which the dancer's personality dissolves and becomes permeable to external influences that become incarnate in him or her.

Curiously enough, in the modern West, music with certain features close to those of ecstatic music is no longer found in places of worship, but in quite different places like discos, where dancers experience the kind of hypnotic isolation that is needed for mystical experience, which—if it were properly directed—could lead to the perception of supersensory realities. The gods are much closer in the exaltation of rock concerts than in the faded canticles of the churches with their well-disciplined chorales, just as vagabond hippies are much closer to the mystical wanderers, the "crazies of god," than frustrated monks snug in their rich monasteries.

Sound levels also play an important role in the effectiveness of hypnotic rites and communication with invisible worlds. Some sound forms of a ritual nature are not meant to be pleasant to the human ear. The "thunderous din" of a ritual nature plays a major role in evoking subtle beings, whether it is the *sarva vadyam* of Indian temples, in which all the instruments are played together, or the din of bells with their strange harmonics, which make people go crazy if they are too close, or yet again the racket of drums in African rites, or of the striking of wooden battens in Buddhist temples or in the monasteries of Mount Athos. The jumble of organ harmonics beneath cathedral vaults often leads to a similar result, creating a tissue of sound that is quite independent of the piece played, through which subtle forces can materialize.

Some forms of religious music do not at all aim at making the gods descend to humankind but merely raise human beings toward the divine, and are in effect forms of melodic meditation. This is the case of music with a mystic character, which remains bound to the spoken word, like the *bhajanas*, those wonderful sung poems evoking divine love and the legends of the gods, whose emotive nature is related to that of secular song.

There are also other forms of solemn music of a secular kind, employed to emphasize ceremonial grandeur. Our masses for full orchestra provide an example and have parallels in all civilizations.

Cosmological Aspects

The second aspect of music is of a cosmological order and has a social character. Such music evokes the structures of the natural world, the cycle of the seasons, the movements of the stars, and seeks to control their impact on human society. Some musical systems attach great importance to this kind of musical influence on social atmosphere.

According to Chinese theory the precision of scales and pitch of the tuning fork influence the balance of society and the prosperity of the country. Such music does not seek to have any psychological impact. It is generally pentatonic in character and denotes movement or energy but only becomes sensitive when it deviates a little from the system. Sounding pipes, used as standards—the *lyu*—were once upon a time carefully preserved in the imperial palace so as to avoid any deviation in the tuning of orchestras, which could have caused disorders, famine, and social conflict.

In the Middle East, the cosmic dances of the Zoroastrians—of which dervish dances are a survival—have the aim of creating an astrologically favorable atmosphere to facilitate the integration of humans with the cosmos. China, India, and the Amerindian civilizations also practiced such ceremonies of an astrological nature.

Owing to its mathematical aspects, music with a cosmological character is related to the yantras, those symbolic diagrams, which also find their application in the interplay of numbers and the proportions that are the basis of the plastic arts. In particular, cosmological music is closely related to the diagrams used as the basis for sacred architecture. The structures of temples, cathedrals, and the homes we live in—their orientation, the positioning of their doors and windows, their proportions and colors—create an environment that has a subtle influence on us. The atmosphere of a cathedral is not a chance effect. On the other hand, the new Vatican audience hall has no more spiritual atmosphere than a garage or a cinema.

The same is valid for the seat of state power. The orientation and proportions of public buildings have an impact on the behavior and attitude of those in them, who have to take serious and consequential decisions. The fact that the French Chamber of Deputies and the Senate are oriented toward the north is not very conducive to the wisdom of the laws promulgated there, since the buildings have not been properly oriented according to the cosmic order.

Much contemporary music tends toward architectural forms, but by neglecting certain fundamental aspects of the significance of sound ratios, it can have a deleterious effect on our balance, on our truthfulness. As with most current social or ethical concepts, these more or less logical developments are based on erroneous postulates and orientations.

What we call modern music can only regain a beneficial role and a human value if it changes not so much its structures as its bases, which—all too often from a cosmological point of view—have to be considered as demoniac, contributing to the moral disorder of our times.

Some forms of musical art, while belonging to the cosmological concept in which the structural element is predominant, have only a weak psychological impact. Some of Bach's works fall into this category.

Psychological Aspects

Music's third aspect is of a psychological nature and concerns the impact of organized sounds on the emotive mechanisms of human beings. Such music can move us to the bottom of our soul, melt our hearts, exalt us.

The music of the Middle East, which derives from Greek music, and the music of India's ragas is constructed on the basis of correspondence of harmonic and psychological factors. Crowd-pleasing martial music belongs to the same family, as also the utilization of sound forms for medical and psychological purposes: music therapy.

From the point of view of psychological impact, the most effective syntax (manner of organizing sounds) is modal. This system predominates in the Middle East and in India, but it was also the basis of the music of the Mediterranean world up to a relatively recent period. This system divides the octave into twelve areas containing the fifty-four sounds that have psychological repercussions, in the form of expressive nuances.

The major peculiarity of the modal system, from the psychological point of view, is its fixed base tone, known as the tonic. This sound, maintained throughout the performance of any mode, means that all the notes chosen for the scale also have a constant pitch, and always correspond to the same frequencies. If a given interval, say a minor third for example, is felt to be associated with a given feeling—such as tenderness or sadness—this feeling will always be represented by the same sound and will be made increasingly acute by repetition.

In India, musical modes are called "ragas," or "states of mind." A raga can also be defined as a theoretical scale, as a set of proportional intervals, or as a complex of sounds, each of which has a psychological impact or precise significance. Taken as a whole, they create an emotive atmosphere or state of mind.

Indian psychology envisages nine different sorts of mood or affective states, which are called *rasas,* "flavors." They are thus linked to numerical factors, giving us an interesting glimpse into the workings of the brain's mechanisms and the nature of our aesthetic and emotional reactions. The emotive atmosphere of the ragas is often associated with those that prevail at different times of day and night, or else of the seasons that punctuate the year's cycle. Like the vegetal world, we react differently in the morning or the evening, in the spring or autumn.

Modal music can only be improvised, since preset forms of melody adversely affect modal consciousness, its internal vision centered on the scale of the mode and the atmosphere it creates. The musician should therefore cruise freely in the inner ambiance created by the mood without ever coming out of it. It is a very intense and a very extraordinary experience, which requires total abstraction from the outer world. In fact, it is a form of meditation that can easily become mystical in character.

The listener is also gradually influenced by the nature of the mode, becoming immersed in a sort of sound bath, which evokes a well-defined feeling. The listener gradually identifies with the emotional scenario evoked. This is why a good performance of modal music can have a profound effect on the audience, making them melancholic, wary, calm, enterprising, aggressive, or tender, according to the atmosphere created by the performer.

In actual fact, any music that seeks to move us—such as what we know as romantic music—requires us to abandon ourselves to the feeling evoked, which takes precedence over technical format. That is why Greek warriors were advised not to listen to certain modes, which stimulate a kind of erotic languor. The Dorian mode was recommended, since it stimulates courage and energy. During the Middle Ages, modes deemed to be sensual were forbidden by the church, always sexophobic, not to speak of the augmented fourth, which does in fact open horizons onto the invisible, and was considered to be diabolical, the *diabolus in musica*.

If we wish to listen to modal music of the Indian kind, we must change our habits a little, and give up any kind of analytical or critical spirit. We must get used to being penetrated, lulled, imbued by the sounds, lose all notion of time, abandon ourselves without reticence to the magical climate that will gradually engulf us. As in yoga meditation, we must silence the useless agitations of our mind. We shall then see gradually opening in front of us an unknown and marvelous musical landscape. This experience is not so very different from those caused by certain drugs but is much richer and susceptible of infinite variety. Music can then become for us a school of wisdom and key to true knowledge, a means of communicating with the invisible, with that mysterious world of genies and gods.

The Secret of the Tantras

The double reality of the physical body and the subtle body merely expresses a particular aspect of cosmological reality. The basic structures of the universe and of the terrestrial world, like those of the human body, have a double aspect, the apparent (matter) and the real (subtle). The earth belongs to the solar system. Nothing can exist on earth that does not, on principle, exist in the solar world. Thus, there must be a solar consciousness, a solar intelligence, a solar life, or else where would these components in human beings have come from?

The solar world and terrestrial world must thus be represented in the same way as in the subtle person. In both cases, we shall encounter centers of energy, critical points at which are located the energies that determine life, consciousness, duration, physical or subtle perceptions of the earth as well as of human beings, and the transcendent powers that we call gods, who are manifest there.

This explains why certain places are sacred, certain regions privileged, a fact that has an impact on the characteristics of the human beings who live in such places. In the same way, certain areas of the human body are the seat of particular faculties. Sacred geography is superadded to the inner geography of the world and human beings. They are complementary, and in no way contradictory.

Any attempt at communication between states or levels of different beings, between humans, gods, and spirits of all kinds that our rudimentary senses cannot perceive, requires knowledge of the world's subtle structures, which allows us to discover the openings, the secret passages through which we can communicate with other forms of being, other dimensions of space, time, and matter.

The search for this fundamental data that lies at the root of every aspect of the visible and invisible, inert or living worlds is the only true science. It simultaneously implies both faultless logic and unprejudiced intuition. On the one hand, it includes supramental perception cultivated by the introspective methods of Yoga, allowing us to reactivate our non-mental knowledge potential, and on the other an attentive observation of the signs, the parallel elements that we can discern in the most varied forms of manifestation, through which we can distinguish certain constants. In Hindu philosophy, this latter approach—which we may term cosmological—bears the name of Samkhya (numerable), "the observation of constants," and is considered to be the indispensable complement of Yoga (union)—supramental perception, whose observations it controls and explains.

Once certain keys indicated by the constants and basic structural elements have been determined, we can utilize the fundamental energies that are the very basis of life to try to establish communication between the various states of being—the gods, spirits, the dead—beings that are not usually perceptible in the dimension that determines the barriers of our senses and the limits of apparent relative time, which depends on our perception of duration. This communication is established with the aid of three practical and interdependent methods called:

mantras (magical formulas)
yantras (magical diagrams)
tantras (magical gestures or acts)

These three elements of the communication system between worlds are closely linked to one another and are inseparable in action. Such methods of magical action may appear absurd and irrational from the point of view of our habitual logic, but they are based on absolute realities, which only the most abstract aspects of modern science are occasionally beginning to point out for us.

The universe is divine thought, perceived as an apparent reality, but what is thought if not a ratio of forces? There is no thought without existence, no existence without a material support. Thought-matter-life form an indissoluble triangle. The language we use to try to grasp and communicate our thought approximately is made up of a very limited number of symbolic elements, formed by around fifty articulated sounds, which we do our best to combine to give our ideas an approximate delimitation. Mantras pick up these basic elements, and yantras allow us to establish the corresponding geometric diagrams.

For any given world to exist, the conditions that make it possible must first exist. The first stage in any world is thus potential *(avakasha)*. For the spatial world, such potential depends on the existence of space, which is one of the properties of a subtle element called ether *(akasha)*.

Space, however, has no dimension except in relation to an element of measurement, a vibration, a given wavelength. In humans, this vibration is called the "alpha" rhythm of the brain, which determines the duration, or dimension of time *(kala)*.

For beings existing on a wavelength that is very different from our own, a second of their time may correspond to a thousand years of ours. Or, on the contrary, a second of our time may last centuries for them. In both cases, they can only be perceptible to us if we can escape from duration, from the limitations of our perception of time.

Vibration is a form of energy. The world's substance can always be reduced to ratios of energy elements. Energy is the tension that exists between two opposing forces. In the spatial world, these two forces appear as a concentrating centripetal force that gives rise to energy coagulations, such as stars or atoms, and a dispersive centrifugal force that tends to dissolve and break up, to disperse and destroy a world in perpetual expansion.

Centripetal force corresponds to the protector principle called Vishnu, while the centrifugal force of the destroyer principle is called Shiva. It is this latter principle that triumphs in an atomic explosion. The movement of stars and atoms is the resultant balance of these two tendencies. This resultant is called Brahma (size) in its cosmological aspect, or Shakti (energy) in its energy aspect. These principles are found in an indefinite number of increasingly complex forms in all things. They are expressed by three tendencies: sattva, the constructive or ascendant tendency (Vishnu); tamas, the destructive or descending tendency (Shiva); and rajas, the tendency of orbital movement and action (Brahma).

Each tendency recreates the contrast of opposites, considered as being male (Shiva) and female (Shakti-Vishnu). Each material element, each being or god, is again divided into an equilibrium of opposites. Every principle and every god is thus represented with a counterpart or goddess.

Among the cosmological factors that characterize opposites, we may observe that at the basis of what we term male we find an "odd" factor, and at the basis of whatever we call female an "even" factor. This is starting to appear in modern genetics.

The basic elements required for the formation of atoms, life, and thought could be symbolized by verbal (vibratory) formulas or structural (geometric) formulas. From a verbal point of view, we say that the Creator utters the universe: creation by the Word. Since vibration is assimilated to sound, a world where all is vibration can be represented by sound ratios, mantras, or "magic formulas." At the same time, creation can be envisaged as a structure, that is, ratios of forces that can be expressed by numbers or symbolized as diagrams, the yantras, or "magic figures."

At the level of life, creation may be represented by the sexual act, as well as by symbolic gestures, the mudras. The magical aspect of ritual acts is called *tantra*.

Mantras, yantras, and tantras are interdependent. Through them communication is possible between the different levels of existence. They are at the basis of all religion, any approach to the real and the supernatural. Here there is no hiatus between physics and metaphysics, material and subtle, psychology and parapsychology.

Yantras are diagrams representing the inner structure of things, those basic formulas of creation that are found in all aspects of the world and, from one level of existence, allow us to communicate with another, from mineral to vegetable, to animal, to human, to the suprasensory (spirits and genies), to the supernatural (the gods), to the transcendent (the Absolute). They are linked to sound formulas (mantras) that are indicated by symbolic letters. They are the basis for any communication with the invisible, for all magic rites or tantras, for all temple architecture, or any anthropomorphic representation of the gods.

TANTRIC MANTRAS

Tantric mantras comprise a single syllable corresponding to the symbolic elements of articulation.

The mantra that corresponds to the fire triangle is the syllable AUM, which contains the entire articulated language, since it is formed of the guttural "A," the labial "U" and the cerebral "M." All other possibilities of articulation are found within this triangle.

Besides the syllable AUM, which is of a universal nature, Tantric mantras all present certain common sound features. They may be grouped together in complex formulas or embodied in linguistic expressions, since by themselves they never form "words" of the ordinary language. Mantras corresponding to certain energy aspects represented by yantras are indicated by syllabic characters. Indeed, no yantra is complete, nor can it be employed for magical purposes, unless it is accompanied by its corresponding mantras and appropriate mudras, symbolic acts or gestures. The sign of the cross is a mudra representing the primacy of the male element (vertical) over the female element (horizontal), the primacy of the fire that mounts and rises to heaven over the water that tends toward leveling out, equalization, and inaction.

The main elements in Tantric mantras are the following:

LANG, the basic seed *(dhara bija)*
VANG, the seed of the lord of the waters *(Varuna bija)*
RANG, the seed of fire *(vahni bija)*
YANG, the seed of the wind *(vayu bija)*
HANG, the seed of ether *(akasha bija)*

KLING, the seed of desire *(kama bija)*
KRING, the seed of death *(kali bija)*
SHRING, the seed of fortune *(Lakshmi bija)*
HRING, the primordial power *(mula mantra)*
PHAT, mantra of the sword that separates the subtle from the gross
HUNG, the offering

These mantra elements are combined with words that have an esoteric meaning to create more or less complex magical formulas. They include expressions such as *aham sah* (I am That), the mantra identifying the microcosm with the macrocosm, which we unconsciously pronounce with every breath.

Tantrism moreover utilizes ordinary words, giving them a particular symbolic meaning. The ritual texts and formulas of Tantrism cannot therefore be understood or utilized without possessing the key. For example:

bindu (the "limit point" separating the nonmanifest from the manifest) means "sperm"
vajra (lightning) means "the male organ"
mudra (the gesture) means "vaginal secretions"
padma (the lotus) means "the woman."

Mudras are gestures, movements, contractions, or postures of the body that make it possible to reach certain limit points within the human structure that can be used as openings, passages from one order of existence to another. They are the key to our possibilities of communicating with the suprasensory or extrasensory world.

Some gestures are purely physical and correspond to mantras (sound symbols), or yantras (geometric symbols), but Yoga mudras are more complex, allowing us to force the secret doors concealed within the human structure, through which we can communicate with other worlds.

The main mudras defined by Yoga treatises number twenty-five and their utilization is essential for any magical or Tantric realization.

THE SUBTLE STRUCTURES OF HUMAN BEINGS

Human beings are the culmination, the raison d'être of creation. They are robots of prodigious complexity, which—through an autonomous consciousness—in some way perceive the Creators' work from outside, thus giving it reality, since a creation that is not perceived, that has no witnesses, does not exist.

Each divine dream, each picture conceived by the Creator needs a spectator to witness its reality. For this particular world, we are the witnesses. The limitations of our perceptions lend an apparent truth to an illusory universe, since what we perceive as objects are, in actual fact, merely conglomerations of atoms, centers of pure energy evolving in abysses of infinitesimal emptiness.

The human robot is a complex mechanism whose energy centers develop into living cells, vital energies, sensory potential, mechanisms of autonomous thought, and consciousness. If we strip down this mechanism, discover and study the various workshops that together constitute a living being, we reach the very sources of existence, of life and consciousness, and we can eventually utilize their latent potentials, which—at a certain level—are practically limitless.

Exploring these secret potentials requires a very strict method involving the coordination of physical, vital, and mental elements. This method is called Yoga and it allows us to explore ourselves and analyze the nature of the various centers that process our faculties, our substance, our modes of perception, our vital energies, and our genetic code.

In the human body, the centers of consciousness—its faculties and various powers, examined during the course of Yoga introspection—appear as yantras. The centers in which our various energies are located are called *chakras* (wheels) or *padmas* (lotuses). By becoming familiar with the structure of the various chakras and exploring their various mechanisms, we can develop our latent faculties and powers. The chakras of the subtle body are the basic structures of the human being. The form of the physical body is merely a gross covering, while the senses, owing to their narrow limitations, are actually barriers to any true perception of the real.

Yantras are not arbitrary symbols. They are the most precise representation of creation's basic structures, at the level of matter, or at the level of life and thought. They explain the process through which the Creator fashions the world. They are the blueprints of the universe and of humankind. Exploring some of them by introspection in the chakras of the subtle body allows us to control all our centers of life and thought, to develop real powers and faculties, to control and utilize all our latent forces and to act on ourselves and on the world around us, to practice levitation, change the duration of time, to see the past and future, to go to any terrestrial or superterrestrial location, to leave this dimension and see the structure of atoms or of solar systems. The definitions of Hindu science concerning the structure of atoms or solar systems are based on such observations.

At the base of yantra structure, we find certain symbolic elements that have a universal value, such as the fire triangle, the water triangle, and the star pentagon, the crescent moon of the fifth day. We also encounter:

The star hexagon, which represents union, creative power, pleasure, perfection, universality, space, the orbital tendency (rajas), creation, movement.

The square, which represents the earth. All terrestrial life is governed by the number 4: seasons, castes, the ages of life, the directions of space, the dwellings of humankind.

The circle, which symbolizes the worlds. Each universe contained in another is represented by a circle. The small inner circle represents the emptiness that is inside and outside all things.

CHAKRAS

Any living being is formed of two intermixing and apparently conflicting structures: On the one hand, a physical body with a mental component culminating in the brain, logical thought, and communication, and, on the other, a subtle energy body controlling all our vital energies, which is responsible for our intuitive perception. This secret body escapes the control of our mental faculties and is our true being. It is inserted in our visible being and is inverse to it. Its central point is at the base of the spine in the region of our sexual organs, which is the noble, essential part of our being. By a great effort of introspection, after reducing to silence the incessant chattering of our mental apparatus, we can gradually explore this secret part of ourselves. One after the other, we discover the functional centers of this vital being who dwells in our visible body. These centers are called chakras (wheels) and are in actual fact the systems that operate our vital mechanisms and open for us the access to the sources of life, true knowledge, to the universes that surround us together with their inhabitants, the gods, genies, fairies, spirits, demons, the whole subtle world that teems around us and that we can only perceive by this means.

During this inner journey, the chakras appear to us as yantras, the diagrams associated with mantras, or sound formulas. They correspond to what we may term magical powers, since they are beyond the capacity of our visible body. This is the very basis of tantras, or magical acts. In the chakras, we also find the different degrees of transcendent powers that we call gods.

Descriptions of the chakras provided by the inner experience of yogis show certain constants, as well as—quite often—gaps and even slight differences, deriving from the degree of precision with which the yogi describes the inner journey.

Chakras are represented as open lotus flowers, their "petals" being oriented regions in which certain powers or faculties are centralized. During a yogi's inner journey, it is—by way of example—by penetrating the second bottom left petal of the third chakra that the yogi discovers the power of levitation.

One Tantric Yoga manuscript describing the chakras starts (reading upward from the bottom) with a list of 135 fundamental principles, which—according to Hindu cosmological concepts—form the basis of the structures of the universe. The list begins with the conscious being, perception, inaction, name, form, reality, consciousness, enjoyment, totality, the abstract, the beginning, growth, decline, causality, destruction, and so on and ends with localization, support, emptiness, vacuum, and universality. It passes through the five senses, the five elements, the notions of consciousness, individuality, life, different vital energies, and so on.

Then comes a list of the seven worlds, each with its three divisions: heavenly worlds, infernal worlds, and worlds of the living. This is followed by descriptions of the various levels of the particular creation on which human existence lies.

First is a primordial energy called the power of the frog *(darduri)*. By meditating on the frog, we acquire the power of conveying ourselves instantly to any point of space. There follows the principle of time, the destroyer, bearing a red standard and a lotus flower. Then Shiva appears in his causal aspect, armed with a trident, followed by the principle of protective energy, bearing the attributes of Vishnu.

From the word and mind of the primordial being came forth the tortoise, on which the world rests. The tortoise—showing itself openly or withdrawing into its shell—is the symbol of the limit point at which manifestation appears openly or vanishes, closed up within itself. Next the lower world develops, peopled with mythical beings called snakes. Higher up is Vishnu in the form of a wild boar, in which guise he lifts the world above the waters of the primordial ocean. Superposed circles represent the seven worlds.

The first of the subtle centers within the human body is "the Base" *(adhara chakra)*, located in the region of the anus. It has four petals representing the powers of the coiled energy. In the center is the five-faced god Shiva, the principle of life. On his knees appears Ganapati, the elephant god, symbol of the fundamental identity of macrocosm and microcosm, of human and god. Ganapati is accompanied by his two wives, Success (Siddhi) and Intelligence (Buddhi). The magic syllable that corresponds to this center is the character LANG.

The second center, "Support of Individuality" *(svadhishthana chakra)* is located at the root of the genitals, where the gods Brahma, the creator, and the principle of the waters, Varuna, reside. This center has six petals. The goddess Savitri (hymn to the sun), Brahma's daughter, rests on the god's knees. The magic formula found in the center is the character VANG, the principle of the waters.

The coiled energy located at the base of the spine is presented as the third center, although it can only be reached through one of the previous centers. This power, known as "the Power of the Snake" is the principle of life and consciousness itself. The solar and lunar energy circuits (male and female), which govern the right and left sides of body and brain respectively, start from here.

The fourth center, "the Jewel City" *(manipura chakra),* is found in the region of the navel. There is the goddess of fortune (Shri, Shakti), bearing in her heart Rudra, the lord of tears, and the divine vulture, Garuda. This is the center of the fire principle, whose magic syllable is RANG.

The heart is presented here as a lotus-shaped center with nine petals, although it can only be controlled starting from the next center.

The sixth center, located close to the heart, is that of "Inaudible Sound" *(anahata chakra).* The god Shiva in his eternal form resides here with Uma, his partner, and the golden fetus *(hiranya garbha),* the origin of the world. This is the birthplace of the sacred syllable AUM. The center of life and vital breath, it is the dwelling of the breathing principle and the magic syllable of air, YANG.

The seventh center is the center of "Great Purity" *(vishudda chakra),* located in the throat. The goddess of Not-Knowing (Avidya) reigns over the seventh center, wearing a necklace of human skulls. Virata, the cosmic Being, in his hermaphroditic guise (Ardhanarishvara), who creates the world through his dance, resides in her heart. This lotus has forty-four petals. Corresponding to the principle of ether, whose magic syllable is HANG, this center is the door of liberation, through which the yogi can perceive the past and future.

The center of "Enjoyment" *(dalana)* is located in the face, where our senses of perception are concentrated. The face is here called the "Upper Circle" and the "witness of the inner faculties, the notion of individuality and the twenty-five principles." It is the meeting point of the three subtle arteries, *ida, pingala,* and *sushumna.*

Between the eyebrows is the center of "Command" *(ajna chakra)*, which is where the third eye is located, through which all reality is perceived beyond the limits of space and time. Its deity is the principle of Time *(mahakala)* and Death. This center controls the mental functions.

Next we reach the center of "Fire" *(agneya chakra)* with its two petals. There dwells the Supreme Lord, Paramatma. This is where the subtle body's central artery, known as sushumna, ends; through it the yogi—by the force of his power—makes the coiled energy rise.

On the forehead is located the center of "Nectar," whose cup is the moon and whose symbol is the cow of abundance.

The eleventh center is the "Lotus of the Thousand Petals, the center of Immortality," which is located at the top of the cranium. Here resides the Guru, the power of knowing *(chaitanya shakti)*, as well as the mantra of identity "I am That" (aham sah). Here dwells the lord of desire (Kama natha) and his lover, and here, too, all the faculties dissolve into the Absolute.

Above is the double triangle of "Transcendent Energy," with the magic syllable of ether, HANG, at its center, while higher up still is the Linga, the phallus, the divine object of all knowledge gripped in its receptacle, the image of the female principle through which it is manifest in humans and in the universe.

Shaivism and the Primordial Tradition

An element of consciousness acts as a kind of inactive witness in every atom or conglomerate of atoms, in every cell, as well as at the center of the "inner organ" *(antahkarana),* the principal engine of every living being. This inner organ comprises three faculties: the mental *(manas),* which thinks; intelligence *(buddhi),* which comprehends, chooses, and recalls; and the sense of individuality or self *(ahamkara),* which allows each entity to affirm its independence, or difference. The fourth element contained in the inner organ—as in all other individual structures—is a fragment of consciousness *(chit).* However, this consciousness does not really "belong" to the inner organ, since it is inseparable from Universal Consciousness, just as the space contained in an urn is only apparently and temporarily separated from the immensity of space in which it loses its identity once the urn is broken. This total consciousness, of which a fragment appears—as it were—imprisoned in all beings, is sometimes called the universal soul *(atman).* In actual fact, the individual soul has no autonomy at all, since it is not really separated from omnipresent total consciousness.

The world garden is marvelous for its harmony, its fantasy, the beauty of its structures, the variety of its forms, its plants, the beasts of all sorts that live in it and are its ornaments, as well as its spectators, who perceive and enjoy its incredible beauty. Through the consciousness present in all creatures, the Absolute Being contemplates its work and delights in it.

This perception and admiration of the world takes place at two different levels. Among animals it is merely aesthetic perception and enjoyment, but in human beings it can develop into an analytical comprehension of the structures and harmonies that are the secret of the beauty of beings and things. In this, the development of knowledge *(shana)* plays an essential role. This second step in perceiving the world, involving an understanding of its structures, is the superior stage in perceiving the Creator's work.

The game *(lila)* by which the Creator principle enjoys its creation through witnesses who contemplate it and take part in it reveals the double function of living beings, which is perception and knowledge. These functions are usually divided between two categories of beings, apparently independent, but profoundly linked, which are animals and spirits, whereas they are united in the double nature of the human being.

Animals and plants are in some way the visible part of subtle beings, spirits, genies, and gods, which govern and inhabit them. We can often make contact with the spirits through their vegetal or animal twin. This is why certain animals and trees are considered sacred. Through the respect and love we bear them, as well as their worship, we attract the benevolence of the subtle spirits, genies, and fairies that are their invisible twins, governing the aspects of the natural world.

In this dualism of subtle spirits and animals, perception and knowledge functions are separated. In the human being, the divine game unites these two aspects; the human animal gradually develops an aptitude for knowledge, having in some way absorbed its subtle double, or guardian angel. This is why the human species bears a double heritage: its genetic, or physical heritage, which perceives external forms and delights in them, but is also part of the scenario; and its initiatic heritage of knowledge, the aptitude to gradually comprehend the nature of the world and certain aspects of its structure.

By developing the living body—which is where consciousness dwells—through its perfection, evolution, and genetic progress, it is possible to develop faculties suited to its intuitive role in analyzing the structures of creation, giving rise to forms of knowledge *(vidya)* known as artistic expression and scientific analysis.

At a certain moment in our evolution as human beings, we may develop curiosity about world aspects that are normally perceived only by spirits and gods. We then discover within ourselves the potential of perception beyond the limitations imposed on us by the prison of our senses, allowing us only to perceive external forms, which we share with animals.

THE THREE ELEMENTS OF KNOWLEDGE

In order to carry out our role as witnesses, not only of apparent forms, but of the structures on which the various aspects of the universe are built, we need to develop a triple faculty: a faculty of seeing that is independent of our senses; an analytical faculty of a mathematical kind; and a faculty of externalizing, communicating, a language. This is why, at a given moment in human development, the three methods appear, making the formation and transmission of knowledge possible. These three methods are called Yoga, Samkhya, and Shabda.

In their effort to control and extend their suprasensory perceptions, the seers, or rishis, of the first ages were led to develop Yoga techniques. Through these methods they managed to pass beyond the limitations of the senses and the conditioning of space and time. Thus they managed to see atoms *(anima),* or to contemplate from the outside the cells that form stellar systems and galaxies *(sharima),* which are the organs of the body of Purusha, the Universal Man. By introspection, they also managed to perceive within themselves the relationships of those forces that give birth to life, feeling, and thought.

The second faculty is the faculty of measurement, the mathematical spirit. Any analysis of the structures of the cosmos, as well as of the geometric harmonies that determine the nature of astral or atomic cells, and of the conglomerates that constitute living beings, rests essentially on perception of numerical factors. The word *samkhya* means "number" and is also the term utilized to designate cosmology, which is the study of the countable, the measurable, since, in the universe, everything is ultimately of a geometric and harmonic nature.

Language is a system of sound symbols—words—allowing forms

of thought to be grasped and then externalized. It is thus a means of expression and communication for Yoga perceptions and the analyses made through Samkhya.

VISION AND WORD

Like the substratum of thought, the seers' perception is by nature a vision *(pashyanti)*. But it is through the Word, by the audible structures *(vaikhari)* of language, that the vision is externalized and communicated. This is why the birth of the world, as the materialization of creative thought, is compared to the action of the Word, the externalization of thought or vision. The knowledge tradition potential starts from the moment when the aptitude for language develops.

Language is thus the essential element that differentiates humans from other living species, at least those perceptible to us. In the evolution of life, the birth of Homo sapiens as a species distinct from other animal species, capable of playing a separate role in creation, coincides with the genetic appearance of the faculty of speech, the incarnation of the Word. This is why, in human society, in parallel with genetic transmission that perfects the physical body, the habitat of knowledge, a further, initiatic transmission takes place, thanks to which the visions of the seers of those early ages have been perpetuated through the generations. This transmission constitutes what is termed "tradition" *(parampara)*.

MANVANTARA AND YUGA

In a universe where everything is number (samkhya) and movement *(jagat)*, the evolution and duration of the terrestrial world are determined by numerical factors, cycles connected with the rhythms of the astral cell, of which the Sun is for us the center, whose most visible forms are days, months, and years. Other cycles regulate the life duration of individuals and species.

Seen from the modern view of history, can a date be given to the era when the seers began to formulate what has come down to us as primordial tradition? The only thing we can say is that, since knowledge is part of the raison d'être of humanity, the seers' perception must have occurred when the evolution of the species reached maturity, and when the human being became capable of playing the role of witness. Like a flower that blossoms in due season, perception of the world's secrets appeared in the seers' spirit when humankind reached maturity. We may note that, in actual fact, the seers' perceptions took place simultaneously in various parts of the world, just as nowadays we find the same discoveries appearing at the same time on different continents.

At some levels of knowledge however, aptitude is not simultaneous among all variants of the species, since they are not all at the same level of evolution. The tradition of one group cannot therefore be transferred to another.

The cycle corresponding to the duration of any human species is called *manvantara* (the space of one Manu). The name Manu, the progenitor, means "Man," a term that corresponds to the Semitic "Adam," which has the same meaning. The manvantara is divided into four eras known as Yugas.

During the era known as the Age of Truth (Satya Yuga), Hesiod's Golden Age, the perceptions of the sages or seers (rishis) established the bases of this approach to the world's deep reality, which is the foundation of the primordial tradition, the expression of universal laws *(Sanatana Dharma)*.

The second era, the Age of the Three Ritual Fires (Treta Yuga), saw the constitution of human society, the family, tribe, hierarchy, and royalty. Temporal power was wielded by the king, who by his virtue was responsible for the group's prosperity. The sages, or seers, lived in the forest in contact with nature and the spirits. There was no sacerdotal caste. Domestic rites were performed by all, without any distinction of status. Life became sedentary; agriculture developed. The fire god (Agni), now domesticated, became the center of the family group, the hearth. Relationships between humans and with other species—gods, spirits, animals, and plants—were formalized, in an effort to conform to the universal laws. The search for harmony in human beings' relations with nature, the definition of rites and other means of communicating with the gods, and becoming integrated with the divine work, gave rise to a body of concepts and practices that became known as Shaivism.

The third era, the Age of Doubt (Dvapara Yuga), saw the birth of various mythologies, the philosophical schools, and atheistic doctrines. During this period urban civilizations and the hierarchy of functions developed. Tradition was preserved by wandering ascetics, the *ajivikas* (beggars), the *kalamukhas* (black heads), and the *kapalikas* (wearers of skulls), living outside society.

The onset of the fourth era, the Age of Conflicts (Kali Yuga), saw the appearance of city religions, concerned only with human beings. Humankind has abandoned nature and become the enemy of other species. Religion has been reduced to social codes, ethics. So-called prophets have set up innumerable sects that fight each other. Tradition, transmitted by the initiates, has become esoteric and hidden but is always alive and can reappear when the conditions of the cycle are favorable.

Barbarian invaders, whose incursions everywhere marked the beginning of the current Kali Yuga, imposed their myths and their culture in India, as also in Greece and Rome, forcing the Shaivite-Dionysian tradition to go underground. Hence two parallel traditions appeared: one, which is official (Vedic), and the other, which is secret (Shaivite), thanks to which India manages to preserve the organization that allows the primordial tradition to be transmitted through the initiatic channels of the sannyasis. Some aspects of tradition also exist elsewhere in an esoteric form, despite official religion.

Over the centuries, Shaivism has had a gradual and profound impact on Vedic religion, giving rise to Hinduism. It was, however, only from the fourth century B.C.E., at a time when rediscovered writing made it possible to confront traditions, that transcriptions were made, on the one hand, of the Vedic texts and, on the other, of a mass of documents deriving from the Shaivite tradition, particularly the *Agamas* (traditions), *Tantras* (rules), and *Puranas* (legendary accounts), most of which have still not been analyzed or published, but which living tradition has perpetuated in secret down to our own times.

WRITING

Traditional knowledge was established strictly in the oral domain. Suprasensory perception, analyzed in a mathematical spirit and externalized by word of mouth, was expressed in condensed mnemotechnic formulas, known as "the Approaches" *(Upanishads).*

Visual symbols—that is, the various forms of writing—only begin to be used to fix certain elements of tradition when the evolution of the cycle announces the decline of knowledge. Writing is a kind of external memorandum, which, at a given moment, fixes formulas used as a basis for the transmission of knowledge in verbal form, which can be compared to highly elaborate proverbs.

Artistic expression is the first step in written language, to the extent that it recalls the harmonies of a numerical nature that constitute its beauty. Conceived first in the form of images, or hieroglyphs, writing long remained tied to a verbal externalization (vaikhari) of vision (pashyanti), which is fundamentally thought. It therefore has an essentially approximate character, limited by the vocabulary at the disposal of any particular language.

Language formulated by writing poses the danger of sterilization, although at the same time it opens new possibilities, transferring learning from the domain of visual and intuitive knowledge to that of intellectual and analytical science. But when congealed writing contradicts living tradition, the "idolatry of the book" appears and opposes tradition. The image of a deity in a temple is not the god itself, but a support through which it can be evoked. Idolatry appears when the statue itself is worshipped and not the subtle being it represents. Similarly, blind belief in texts, whether the Vedas, the Bible, the Koran, or any other "sacred book," indicates ignorance of their nature.

The true Veda (from the root *vid* = knowledge) is the name given to the perception of the body of laws that constitute the universe. It is thus the expression of the Sanatana Dharma, the eternal or natural law. This world law has sometimes been improperly confused with the expressions that various traditions have sought to give it.

The texts known as the Vedas are merely attempts made at a given moment to grasp something of the laws that lie at the basis of the structures of matter, life, and the individual or social being and are limited by approximations that characterize all language. The same is true of any form of knowledge, and of all the sciences, which progress from approximation to approximation. As soon as any attempt is made to turn the knowledge of an era into a gospel, the whole discovery is paralyzed. Dogmatism is the very foundation of ignorance *(avidya)*.

Worship of the sacred book, envisaged as a materialization of divine thought, mistakes the symbol for reality and is thus basically idolatry. It is opposed to the very process of the evolution of knowledge, as represented by tradition, and ends up denying it. That is why "religions of the book" rapidly abandon tradition, which then takes refuge in secret forms of initiatic and esoteric transmission.

I had the chance of observing a similar phenomenon with the poet Rabindranath Tagore. His poems were always sung. In the morning, he would gather his disciples and sing to them his new composition, which they learned by heart. Some of them tried to transcribe the words and set down the tune. A few years later, it was the people who had learned the songs from the notes—"the people of the book"—who claimed to hold the true version and opposed those who had inherited the oral tradition, which was nevertheless much more accurate.

It is not that "sacred books" are necessarily absurd. They are simply obsolete as soon as they are created. They represent stages. What are absurd are the "religions of the book" that, in a world in perpetual development, seek to paralyze the evolution of knowledge, that marvelous adventure that is for humans the sinuous path of discovery, which gradually discloses the secrets of the divine nature of the world.

SCIENCE AND TRADITION

Only intensive selection allows the various human lineages to reach the type of physical perfection that constitutes a favorable habitat for the inner organ, that instrument of knowledge through which a human being can fully realize his or her destiny as a witness. This destiny is not quantitative. A few individuals are sufficient, or even one alone, to let the indwelling fragment of Universal Consciousness contemplate its work, admire it, and delight in it.

When the heritage of traditional knowledge is debased, the human intellect seeks other means to penetrate the world's secrets. That is why, in our own time, when the prodigious knowledge of shamans, sorcerers, and sannyasis is tending to disappear, we find that astrophysicists or biologists rediscover certain fundamental principles of the nature of the world, such as the relativity of space and time, and the structures of life, which—although obtained by other methods—match the data given by the teaching of the rishis, the seers.

The direct view of structures provided by Yoga and the intellectual research of science are two methods aimed at a common goal, which is that of allowing the Supreme Principle to admire the plan of its work through the mirror of individual consciousness. That is why discovery is such a source of joy. Science and clairvoyance are two parallel branches of the same effort of knowledge and are not clearly separated. Scientific discoveries, too, are inspired. Their starting point is intuition, an inner light that resembles clairvoyance. Rationalization only takes place later on.

There is no difference between the nature of the perceptions of clairvoyants and the discoveries of scholars; the only differences are in method and limitation. Both paths are totally free of any a priori reasoning, any dogmatism, any belief or religion, any prophet or human character. Clairvoyants and scientists are the tools of Universal Consciousness, which is independent of the bodies in which it dwells, and is amused by such discoveries.

It is through our love for the forms of the visible world, through the joy that it gives us, and by our effort to understand its nature and structures that we realize our role and communicate with the divine that dwells in us.

THE PERMANENCE OF TRADITION

The life of a species follows the same process as for an individual. It has its childhood, maturity, and decline and is eliminated when it ceases to play the role assigned to it in the harmony of creation as a physical species and as a mirror of Universal Consciousness. This is why tradition, even when it is wholly esoteric and hidden, remains indestructible and operational. Invisible initiates from far off inspire the forms of knowledge, the discoveries of science, so that human beings can play their role of witness for the amusement of the Creator. However, when knowledge—instead of being a means for the delectation of the Absolute Being—becomes a tool for the destruction of the divine work, the apprentice sorcerers are eliminated.

The "catastrophes brought about" that will mark the end of the cycle will lead to a long night, after which, Shiva, through his dance, will give birth to a new humankind. New seers will then rediscover with amazement the secrets of the world and will reestablish knowledge for the pleasure of the Absolute Being. Humankind has already disappeared and been reborn six times and each time a reestablished tradition has marked its steps.

APPENDIX

Light on Samkhya and Poetry

by Jean-Louis Gabin

The esoteric knowledge shared with the West by Alain Daniélou was, in fact, the very core of research by poets and thinkers of the Romantic Era in Europe and in modern French literature, in particular Hugo, Baudelaire, and Rimbaud. The part of his works that has a direct bearing on poetry, namely Samkhyan theories, thus throws new light on that poetry, particularly Baudelaire's "Correspondances" and Rimbaud's "Voyelles."

But firstly, what is Samkhya? The Indians may know, but only a few Indian specialists would be able to answer this question in the West. In any case, no one in the field of literary research or comparative poetry—with the exception of René Daumal, whose works, fifty years after his death, are still confidential—has ever, to my knowledge, thought of using these notions to comment on the works of Baudelaire. We should note that this intellectual ignorance is the subject of an essay by Roger Pol Droit, *L'Oubli de l'Inde,* which expresses surprise as to why this discovery has never been made, when all the thinkers of the nineteenth century, from Hegel to Kierkegaard and Goethe, including Nietzsche, considered that the translation of the *Vedas* and the discovery of the *Upanishads* and *Puranas* would, in the twentieth century, produce a revelation comparable to that of the Greek texts during the Renaissance. He also wonders why the departments of philosophy in the universities and great Western schools continue to ignore the traditional speculative thought of India: Nyaya, or logic; Samkhya, or cosmology; and Advaita, nondualism.

Several of Daniélou's works expound the theories of the ancient Samkhya.[1] In *While the Gods Play,* for example, he writes:

> For the Samkhyas, the universe develops starting from elementary formulas . . . expressible in mathematical or geometric terms (in this case known as Yantras), common to all aspects of creation. There is no difference of nature between the formulas at the basis of the structures of the atoms of matter, the order of the stars, the principles of life, or the mechanisms of perception and thought, which are all parallel and interdependent manifestations of energy."[2]

The relation with comparative poetry appears immediately, if one thinks of Baudelaire's rightly famous sonnet "Correspondences"[3] in the *Flowers of Evil,* which in our own time seems much more than a poem and much more than a theory, starting from its very first words. Its splendor contains a kind of message and even a warning for infinite meditation:

In Nature's temple, living pillars rise,
Speaking sometimes in words of abstruse sense;
Man walks through woods of symbols, dark and dense
Which gaze at him with found familiar eyes.

Like distant echoes blent in the beyond
In unity, in a deep darksome way,
Vast as black night and vast as splendent day,
Perfumes and sounds and colors correspond.

Some scents are cool as children's flesh is cool,
Sweet as are oboes, green as meadowlands
—And others rich, corrupt, triumphant, full,

Expanding as infinity expands:
Benzoin or musk or amber that incense,
Hymning the ecstasy of soul and senses.[4]

Much could now be said about this sonnet: First, on the metaphor with which it begins, the reaffirmation of Nature's sacred character, traversed by the "abstruse" or confused words of the forces that have created it. "Confused words" indeed: in the West this message has been obfuscated as Ronsard pathetically proclaimed three centuries earlier, in 1584, in his elegy inspired by the destruction of the forest of Gastine. And it is significant that it was in the mid-nineteenth century—at a time when triumphant mercantilism and materialism considered the natural world merely as raw material for their enterprises—that the voice of poetry was once again raised, putting the world on guard against a final profanation, in an attempted appeal to forgotten wisdom and knowledge.

We may ask ourselves by what means a poem, a vision that is—first and foremost, according to modern theorists of poetry—strictly personal, "original," even "whimsical" (for less indulgent commentators, who wonder whether Baudelaire really did stick to his theory) could so precisely link up with knowledge whose details were unknown in the Europe of his time? Part of the answer was articulated by Baudelaire himself when he said: "Imagination is the most scientific of faculties because it encompasses and understands universal analogy."[5]

Neither the writings of Franciscans and Thomists, nor the works of Swedenborg or Fourier explored by the exegetes of the *Fleurs du Mal* ever go so far in their vision of "universal analogy" as the Samkhya texts revealed by Daniélou to the French-speaking public and later published in translation in the United States. He specifically explores the connections between those theories and literary research in a chapter of *While the Gods Play* entitled "The Nature of Language," from which the following quotations are taken:

> Language, by means of which we are able to materialize thought and describe the apparent world as perceived by our senses, must therefore present to us characteristics analogous to those of the process by which the universe develops. . . . By delving back to the sources of language, and to the process by which thought is transformed into speech we should be able to uncover something of

> the way in which the creative principle that is the divine "Word" is manifest in creation.
>
> The simplest form of vibration that our senses can perceive is the vibration of air, which, within certain limits, we sense as a sound. We can use sound vibration as a starting point and means of comparison for an understanding of the other, more complex vibratory states—whether they concern the structures of matter or nature of life, or the phenomena of perception and thought.
>
> The organ of speech is constituted as a yantra, a symbolic diagram. The palatal vault (like the celestial vault) forms a hemisphere with five points of articulation allowing the emission of five groups of consonants, five main vowels, two mixed vowels, and two secondary vowels, assimilated to the planets.
>
> Likewise in the musical scale, there are five main notes, two secondary ones, and two alternative notes, which are not arbitrary, but correspond to fundamental numerical relationships between the sound vibrations that we find at the basis of all musical systems. Our perception of colors has analogous characteristics."[6]

Such notions are strangely close to certain ideas of Baudelaire when, on the subject of Wagner's music, he establishes a link between "God who articulates the world as a complex and indivisible totality" and "the reciprocal analogy" that lets a sound suggest color, colors suggest a melody, and both sounds and colors translate ideas. There is, however, a further very distinct parallel between Samkhya theories, as expounded by Daniélou, and the poetry of Rimbaud, particularly his sonnet "Voyelles"[7] or "Vowels":

> *A black, E white, I red, U green, O blue: vowels,*
> *I shall tell, one day, of your mysterious origins:*
> *A, black velvety jacket of brilliant flies*
> *Which buzz around cruel smells,*

Gulfs of shadow; E, whiteness of vapours and of tents,
Lances of proud glaciers, white kings, shivers of
cow-parsley;
I, purples, spat blood, smile of beautiful lips
In anger or in the raptures of penitence;

U, waves, divine shuddering of viridian seas,
The peace of pastures dotted with animals, the peace of
the furrows
Which alchemy prints on broad studious foreheads;

O, sublime Trumpet full of strange piercing sounds,
Silences crossed by Worlds and by Angels:
O the Omega, the violet ray of Her Eyes![8]

In discussions, reviews, and critical editions on Rimbaud, a wide variety of propositions are put forward to find the "key" to this sonnet, which has particularly excited the imagination. I feel that nothing serves better than these passages from Alain Daniélou's comments on the Samkhyas:

> Particular vowels are associated with specific colors. Color differences are due to the frequency ratios of light waves, just as musical sounds are defined by the frequency of sound waves. . . . According to Ragunandan Sharma's *Akshara Vijnana*, the fourteen vowels correspond to the following colors:
>
> A = white
> I = red
> U = yellow
> Ë (ri) = bluish-black
> Ò = black, etc.
>
> These vowels and colors correspond to those that characterize the cycles in which new human species are born and die.[9]

Although scholars are undecided about the possibility of initiatic transmission in the case of Rimbaud—who wrote in his *Illuminations:* "where is the old brahman who taught me proverbs?"—he was indisputably in contact with occult circles and had certainly read Eliphas Levi, just as Baudelaire read Swedenborg. This analysis by Jean Biès of Rimbaud's life and work follows such a reading:

> Who could deny that Rimbaud is a "Seer," even though his clairvoyance is clouded by imperfections and reminiscences? Rimbaud is conscious of the mysterious power of words, anxious to go back to the origin of language and, on attaining the vision of it, to reach the state of awakening. Nothing of all this is formulated clearly, but the intention oozes everywhere and in a singular way links the young sixteen-year-old boy of Charleville . . . with the Kavi and Rishi of primordial times. . . .
>
> From a biographical point of view, the element of anarchic violence concealed in Rimbaud should not be overlooked in any possible comparison with India. We know that revolt and destruction are a formidable manifestation of transcendence; we also know that the East makes positive use of them, whereas the West, being incapable of channeling such forces, pitches them against the structures of the contingent world, instead of employing them for the purpose of inner cleansing. This reversal of priorities, this total absence of ritualization, ends by being fatal to those handling such forces without knowing their nature and function properly. In that decadent atmosphere that was his own, Rimbaud appeared as a co-operator in the *nivrtti marga,* the destructive phase of the rotating cycle. With Sade, he is one of the rare adepts, though more intellectual, of the *vama shara,* "the way of the left hand." Through drink, drugs, sexuality and nomadism, his rejection of institutions, his blasphemies, Rimbaud could have gone further than scandalizing the middle class: like the Shaktas, he could have become the reconciler of the shade and light within himself, but he did not do so. The destructive element even ended by taking the upper, leading the poet to

> existential dissolution and scriptural renunciation; and this owing to lack of preparation, lack of training and spiritual guidance. As a self-taught, and as an inexperienced improviser, Rimbaud hazarded himself on the most perilous of paths. His inner potentials did not find in his circumstances the support needed for their development. . . . Rimbaud is our Shaivite, in the wild state.[10]

In fact,[11] nineteenth century France, which marks the triumph of bourgeois hegemony, witnessed a clandestine efflorescence of esoteric research until the materialism and the messianism of the social utopias came to occupy the areas where the former state religion seems to have shut off the pathways of metaphysical research. In the twentieth century, following Proudhonism, Marxism—which is a parody of religion—expressly tried to consolidate the "positive aspects" of the bourgeois revolution, namely: globalization of the market, dictatorship of human over nature, armed conversion of different civilizations, the fight against traditions, and spiritual life labeled as "obscurantism" even in the domain of art.

Thus, in France, during a major part of the twentieth century, even the poetic art had to serve as an auxiliary to modern, nationalist, political, and social ideologies. While on the communists' side, Aragon earned for himself a sinister immortality with his "Ode to the Genial Stalin," on the Christians' side, Claudel wrote verses comparing the parachutists of the French colonial army in Indochina to Archangel Saint Michel's legions thrashing the demons.

In contrast, the writers of the "Grand jeu," René Daumal in particular, became interested in Vedic tradition but did not get access to Shaivism and to Tantra. André Breton was interested in occult sciences but condemned the traditional societies and ultimately the René Guénon approach as well, despite his fascination for it.

Some other dissidents partly rediscovered the pathway opened up by Rimbaud: Yves Bonnefoy with *Douve,* which is a collection full of Gnostic inquiries, or Gilbert Lely, the most concealed among them, who sings "Notre-Dame de Lumière," an erotic poetry of cosmic proportions:

O, luxury of my sperm in the night of thy thighs!
Up over there, the homologous semen of the Milky Way.

Or else:

The unity–queen sparkled
The world proved to itself. Nothing was more sparse.
O hymenean walls, pandects of azur!
O melting pot of an incorruptible alliance

Thou, space, mountains, Sade, future days
The voluptuousness, the verb, in a single diamond.[12]

The mention of Sade, a passionate atheist and anti-Christian writer, shows that the research of most French poets of the twentieth century could not often come out of the confines of a sense of revolt that was perfectly comprehensible. The same was also the case for the American poets, whereas in the nineteenth century the sense of nature as both sensuous and spiritual—such as in Walt Whitman—was on several counts comparable to that of Baudelaire. It was the rebellious Rimbaud who came to have a direct influence on the Beat Generation, particularly the well-known poet Allen Ginsberg, who succeeded in reestablishing ties with India through Tantric Buddhism, quite close to the "left-hand path" of Shaivism. The revolt of the European poets, however, resulted rather in a refusal of all established paths, even secret, a refusal of all cadres, of all masters, of all traditions. This lead to an hypertrophy of the self, to the Luciferian or Promethean overestimation of the ego in which so many poets got stuck like spiders in their own webs.

The type of intellectual confusion cultivated by Breton vis-à-vis his relationship with the incisive clarity of thoughts of Guénon is an indication: As per the analysis of André Coynet, Breton would have:

> . . . all along wanted to *play* on the *language* of Tradition while at the same time denying its *spirit,* which amounts to simply and

> purely denying the Tradition itself, that to the extent of getting confused whenever he talks about it. The following 1948 declaration, [which] causes one to wonder what it means, is one of the proofs: "It is hardly a question of knowing whether or not a strict written or oral tradition could have really extended from Antiquity to modern times (although this is exactly the constant objection of the common man) but a question of identifying whether the works which continue to have an influence on us maintain or not appreciable relationships with this tradition even if impure."[13]

This overestimation of the ego, which darkens the relationship of the most innovative French poets vis-à-vis the sacred, is certainly most directly expressed by René Char in a poem that bears testimony to a poignant nostalgia and also simultaneously to some sort of complacency, to an incapability of discrimination or of humility that can only end up in a spoiled encounter:

> We are not jealous of the gods, we do not serve them, we are not afraid of them. But at the risk of our life, we attest their multiple existence and we get emotional about belonging to their adventurous breed when their souvenir ceases.[14]

But the remains of the occult tradition and whatever still-living spirituality subsisted in our civilization seem to have taken refuge in this "damned" poetry. Who better than the seventeen-year-old Rimbaud can sum up for us the approach to Tantrism itself: "I say we must become clairvoyant, through a long, immense and reasoned deregulation of all our senses"? What text expresses better than his poem *Soleil et chair* the life-giving nostalgia for the Golden Age and its past reality?

These poetic intuitions, heirs of a persecuted tradition, are answered by the theories of Shaivite cosmology and the *Tantras,* so eloquently given voice to by Alain Daniélou.

Notes

Introduction to Alain Daniélou

1. Alain Daniélou, *The Way to the Labyrinth, Memories of East and West,* Marie-Claire Cournand, trans. (New York: New Directions, 1987).
2. Daniélou, *The Way to the Labyrinth,* 7.
3. Alain Daniélou, *Le Bétail des dieux et autres contes gangétiques* (Paris: Editions du Rocher, 1994); Abridged version in English: *Fools of God* (Madras and New York: Hanuman Books, 1998).
4. Alain Daniélou, *Le Tour du monde en 1936* (Paris: Flammarion, 1987).

Editor's Preface

1. Please refer to the Bibliography for publication information.
2. Daniélou, *The Way to the Labyrinth,* 134–36.
3. Noriko Aikawa, booklet of the triple CD, "A Tribute to Alain Daniélou," *Anthology of Indian Classical Music,* UNESCO Collection, Prix Diapason d'Or (Paris: Audivis, 1997).
4. Daniélou, *Le Bétail des dieux et autres contes gangétiques,* 7–8.
5. Most of the translations of original texts made by Alain Daniélou were into French; a few were into English. Please refer to the bibliography for further publication information.
6. Alain Daniélou, *While the Gods Play: Shaiva Oracles and Predictions on the Cycles of History and the Destiny of Mankind* (Rochester, Vt.: Inner Traditions, 1987), 57–59.
7. Note that during the nineteenth and for most of the twentieth centuries, French Indian studies focused almost exclusively on Buddhism, which had disappeared in India twelve centuries earlier. See, for example: Pierre Singaravelou, "*Les indianistes français et le 'Greater India' (fin XIXe*

siècle—1955)," Les Relations entre la France et l'Inde de 1673 à nos jours, directed by Jacques Weber (Paris: Les Indes Savantes, 2002). Even today, there is no Chair of Shaivism at the Collège de France.

8. As the texts were composed over a period of more than fifty years, it is not surprising that there are occasional differences of expression and even apparent contradictions between them, bearing witness to the vital development of Alain Daniélou's thought, even though Alain Daniélou himself revised these new versions between 1990 and 1992. Also, to avoid repetitions, certain parts of the original texts have been eliminated or integrated.
9. See Emanuela Kretzulesco-Quaranta, *Les Jardins de songe, Poliphile et la mystique de la Renaissance* (Paris: Les Belles lettres, 1986).
10. Philip Rawson, *Tantra, le culte indien de l'extase* (Paris: Le Seuil, 1973).
11. Mircéa Eliade, *Le Yoga, immortalité et liberté* (Paris: Payot, 1954).
12. Henri Corbin, *"Alchimie et archetypes," Eranos* 18 (Zurich, 1950).
13. This Preface was taken in part from the paper presented at the Second Congress of the Association of Indian teachers of French, in 13 December 1998 at Pondicherry, with the title: "L'oeuvre de passeur d'Alain Daniélou" (The Ferryman's Task of Alain Daniélou).

The Shaivite Revival from the Third to the Tenth Centuries C.E.

1. See Stella Kramrisch, *The Presence of Shiva* (New York: Princeton, 1980) (Note by Daniélou).

The Symbolism of the Linga

1. *Shiva Purana*, 1.16.106. This and all other unattributed translations from Sanskrit and Tamil texts are by Alain Daniélou into French; Kenneth Hurry into English.
2. *Linga Purana*, 1.3.2–3.
3. *Ibid.*, 1.3.3–4.
4. *Shiva Purana*, 1.16.106–197.
5. Swami Karpatri, *Lingopasana Rahasya,* published as *The Inner Significance of Linga-worship,* Shiva Sharan–Alain Daniélou, trans. (Calcutta: *Journal of Indian Society of Oriental Art,* vol. 9, 1941), 154.
6. Swami Karpatri, *Lingopasana Rahasya,* 153.
7. *Shiva Purana.*

8. Swami Karpatri, *Lingopasana Rahasya,* 163.
9. Swami Karpatri, *Lingopasana Rahasya,* 154.
10. *Skanda Purana.*
11. Swami Karpatri, *Lingopasana Rahasya,* 158.
12. *Chandogya Upanishad,* 2.13.1.
13. *Purusha Sukta, Rig Veda* 10.90.1.
14. *Shiva Purana,* 1.21.22.
15. *Narada Pancharatra,* 3.1.
16. *Samkhya Karika.*
17. *Shiva Purana,* 1.21.23.24–26.
18. *Linga Purana, Kothi Rudra Samhita,* chap. 12.
19. *Shiva Purana.*

Shaivism and Third Nature

1. *Kanda Puranam.*
2. Mircéa Eliade, *Mephistopheles and the Androgyn* (New York: Sheed and Ward, 1965).

The Nature of Beauty According to the Samkhya

1. Alain Daniélou, *The Hindu Temple, Divinization of Eroticism* (Rochester, Vt.: Inner Traditions, 2001).

Appendix: Light on Samkhya and Poetry

1. Alain Daniélou, *Shiva and Dionysus* (Rochester, Vt.: Inner Traditions, 1984); *While the Gods Play: Shaiva Oracles and Predictions on the Cycles of History and the Destiny of Mankind* (Rochester, Vt.: Inner Traditions, 1987).
2. Daniélou, *While the Gods Play,* 60.
3. "Correspondances":

   La Nature est un temple où de vivants piliers
   Laissent parfois sortir de confuses paroles ;
   L'homme y passe à travers des forêts de symboles
   Qui l'observent avec des regards familiers.

   Comme de longs échos qui de loin se confondent
   Dans une ténébreuse et profonde unité

Vaste comme la nuit et comme la clarté
Les couleurs, les parfums et les sons se répondent.

Il est des parfums frais comme des chairs d'enfants,
Doux comme les hautbois, verts comme les prairies
Et d'autres corrompus, riches et triomphants

Ayant l'expansion des choses infinies
Comme l'ambre, le musc, le benjoin et l'encens
Qui chantent les transports de l'esprit et des sens.

Charles Baudelaire, *Les Fleurs du Mal* (Paris: Editions Garnier-Flammarion, 1959), 13.

4. Charles Baudelaire, *Flowers of Evil,* trans. Jacques Leclerc (Mount Vernon: Peter Pauper Press, 1958), 8.
5. Charles Baudelaire, Letter to Alphonse Toussenel, January 21, 1856, in *Oeuvres complètes, Correspondance générale,* vol. 1, 1833–1856 (Paris: Gallimard, 1973), 336.
6. Daniélou, *While the Gods Play,* 227–35.
7. "Voyelles":

A noir, E blanc, I rouge, U vert, O bleu : voyelles,
Je dirai quelque jour vos naissances latentes :
A, noir corset velu des mouches éclatantes
Qui bombinent autour des puanteurs cruelles,

Golfes d'ombre ; E, candeurs des vapeurs et des tentes,
Lances des glaciers fiers, rois blancs, frissons d'ombelles ;
I, pourpres, sang craché, rire des lèvres belles
Dans la colère ou les ivresses pénitentes ;

U, cycles, vibrements divins des mers virides,
Paix des pâtis semés d'animaux, paix des rides
Que l'alchimie imprime aux grands fronts studieux ;

O, Suprême Clairon plein des strideurs étranges,
Silences traversés des Mondes et des Anges:
O l'Oméga, rayon violet de Ses Yeux !

Arthur Rimbaud, *Œuvres complètes* (Paris: Gallimard, "Bibliothèque de La pléiade," 1979), 53.

8. Arthur Rimbaud, "Vowels," *Collected Poems,* trans. Oliver Bernard (London: Penguin Classics, 1987).
9. Alain Daniélou, *While the Gods Play,* 252.
10. Jean Biès, *Littérature française et pensée hindoue* (Paris: Klincksieck, 1992), 131–32.
11. The text, from this paragraph to the eighth ("These poetic intuitions . . ."), was translated by V. Rajagopalan.
12. *O luxe de mon sperme dans la nuit de tes cuisses !*
Là-haut, la semence homologue de la Voie Lactée. (from "La sertisseuse du cri")
O murs hyménéens, pandectes de l'azur !
O creuset d'une alliance incorruptible !
Toi, l'espace, les monts, Sade, les jours futurs,
La volupté, le verbe, en un seul diamant. (from "Parlant à sa personne")

Gilbert Lely, *Poésies complètes,* vol. 1, critical edition of J. L. Gabin, preface by Yves Bonnefoy (Paris: Mercure de France, 1990–2000), 67, 85.

13. André Coynet, "L'œuvre de Guénon dans la seule perspective qui l'explique," *René Guénon, Les Dossiers H.* (Lausanne: L'Age d'Homme, 1984), 46.
14. *Pause au Château-cloaque*
Nous ne jalousons pas les dieux, nous ne les servons pas, ne les craignons pas, mais au péril de notre vie nous attestons leur existence multiple, et nous nous émouvons d'être de leur élevage aventureux lorsque cesse leur souvenir.

René Char, *Œuvres complètes,* "Le Nu perdu," texte 8 (Paris: N.R.F. Gallimard, Collection "La pléiade," 1985), 427.

Origin of the Texts

Shaivite Cosmology and Polytheism *(Cosmologie shivaïte et polythéisme).* Unpublished, Conference at Aix-en-Provence, 17 May 1982.

The Shaivite Revival, from the Third to the Tenth Centuries C.E. *(Le renouveau shivaïte du IIIe au Xe siècles).* Unpublished, Conference at Venice, November 1981.

The Symbolism of the Linga. Unpublished in English; published in Italian under the title "Il Volto di Shiva," *F.M.R.* 16, September 1983.

The Three Doors *(Les trois portes).* Preface for J. Grand, *Érotisme et Mystique,* Paris, 1984.

Shaivism and Third Nature *(Shivaisme et Troisième nature).* Unpublished, April 1986.

Insights into Initiation *(Apercus sur l'initiation).* Unpublished, Conference at the Grand Lodge of France, Paris, December 1976.

The Science of Dreams *(La science des rêves).* Unpublished, 1984.

Poetry and Metaphysics *(Poésie et métaphysique).* Published under the title "La poésie sacrée hindoue," *La Révolution Intérieure*, 4, Paris, 1982.

The Cock *(Le coq).* Unpublished comments on an article by M. D. Dubois, "Le coq et le soleil," *Historia,* 442.

The Nature of Beauty According to the Samkhya *(Nature de la beauté d'après le samkhya).* Unpublished, January 1985.

Music: The Language of the Gods *(Musique hommes et dieux)*. Unpublished, Conference at Marseille, May 1982.

The Secret of the Tantras *(Le secret des Tantra)*. Introduction to *Le Congrès du Monde*. Milano: Franco Maria Ricci Editore, 1975.

Shaivism and the Primordial Tradition *(Shivaïsme et Tradition primordiale)*. Unpublished, September 1986.

Related Works by Alain Daniélou

A Brief History of India. Kenneth Hurry, trans. Rochester, Vt.: Inner Traditions, 2003.

The Complete Kama Sûtra. Rochester, Vt.: Inner Traditions, 1994.

The Congress of The World. John Shepley, trans. Parma: Franco Maria Ricci Editore, 1981.

The Game of Dice (modified version of the *Contes Gangétiques*) in *The Fourth Ghost Book*. James Turner, ed. London: Pan Books, Barrie & Rockliff, 1965; also translated as *Fools of God*. Madras, New York: Hanuman Books, 1988.

Hindu Polytheism. New York: Bollingen Foundation, 1964; reprinted as *The Gods of India*. Rochester, Vt.: Inner Traditions, 1985; and *The Myths and Gods of India*. Rochester, Vt.: Inner Traditions, 1991, 2004.

The Hindu Temple, Deification of Eroticism. Kenneth Hurry, trans. Rochester, Vt.: Inner Traditions, 2001.

India: A Civilization of Differences. Preface by Jean-Louis Gabin, ed. Kenneth Hurry, trans. Rochester, Vt.: Inner Traditions, 2005.

Introduction to the Study of Musical Scales. London: The India Society, 1943; reissued London: Oriental Books, 1943; New Delhi: Munshiram Manoharlal, 1979; reprinted as *Music and the Power of Sounds, The Influence of Tuning and Intervals in Consciousness*. Introduction by Sylvano Bussoti. Rochester, Vt.: Inner Traditions, 1995.

Manimekhalai, The Dancer with the Magic Bowl by Merchant-Prince Shattan. Translated from the Tamil with the collaboration of T. V. Gopala Iyer and Kenneth Hurry. New York: New Directions, 1989.

Northern Indian Music. London: Christopher and Johnson and Calcutta: Visva Bharati, 1949–1953; London: Halcyon Press, under the auspices of UNESCO, 1954; London: Barrie and Rockliff, 1955, 1968; reprinted as *The Ragas of Northern Indian Music.* Berlin, in collaboration with the International Institute for Comparative Music Studies, 1967; and New Delhi: Munshiram Manoharlal, 1980.

The Phallus, Sacred Symbol of Male Creative Power. Rochester, Vt.: Inner Traditions, 1995, 2001.

Sacred Music, Its Origins, Powers, and Future. Traditional Music in Today's World. Preface by Jean-Louis Gabin, ed. Kenneth Hurry, trans. Varanasi: Indica Books, 2003.

Shilappadikaram, The Ankle Bracelet by Prince Ilangô Adigal. Translation from the Tamil with the collaboration of R. S. Desikan. New York: New Directions, 1965; India: Penguin Classics, 1993.

Shiva and Dionysus. Kenneth Hurry, trans. London and The Hague: East-West Publications, 1982; reprinted as *Shiva and Dionysus, the Omnipresent Gods of Transcendence and Ecstasy.* Rochester, Vt.: Inner Traditions, 1984; and *Gods of Love and Ecstasy.* Rochester, Vt.: Inner Traditions, 1992.

Le Shiva Svarodaya, Ancien Traité des Présages et Prémonitions d'après le souffle vital. Preface by Jean Varenne. Milano: Arché, 1982.

Virtue, Success, Pleasure and Liberation, Traditional India's Social Structures, The Four Aims of the Life in the Tradition of Ancient India. Rochester, Vt.: Inner Traditions, 1993.

The Way to the Labyrinth, Memories of East and West. Marie-Claire Cournand, trans. New York: New Directions, 1987.

While the Gods Play, Shaiva Oracles and Predictions on the Cycle of History and the Destiny of Mankind. Barbara Bailey, Michael Baker, and Deborah Lawlor, trans. Rochester, Vt.: Inner Traditions, 1987, 2003.

Yoga, Method of Reintegration. London: Johnson, 1949, 1951, 1954; reprinted New York: University Books, 1973; reprinted as *Yoga, Mastering the Secrets of Matter and the Universe.* Rochester, Vt.: Inner Traditions, 1991.

Web site: www.alaindanielou.org

Index

BOOKS OF RELATED INTEREST

The Myths and Gods of India
The Classic Work on Hindu Polytheism from
the Princeton Bollingen Series
by Alain Daniélou

Gods of Love and Ecstasy
The Traditions of Shiva and Dionysus
by Alain Daniélou

While the Gods Play
Shaiva Oracles and Predictions on
the Cycles of History and the Destiny of Mankind
by Alain Daniélou

A Brief History of India
by Alain Daniélou
Translated by Kenneth F. Hurry

The Complete Kama Sutra
The First Unabridged Modern Translation of
the Classic Indian Text
Translated by Alain Daniélou

India: A Civilization of Differences
The Ancient Tradition of Universal Tolerance
by Alain Daniélou

Shiva
The Wild God of Power and Ecstasy
by Wolf-Dieter Storl, Ph.D.

Yoga Spandakarika
The Sacred Texts at the Origins of Tantra
by Daniel Odier